CONSUMER CHOICE

MACMILLAN STUDIES IN MARKETING MANAGEMENT

General Editor: Professor Michael J. Baker
University of Strathclyde

This series is designed to fill the need for a compact treatment of major aspects of marketing management and practice based essentially upon European institutions and experience. This is not to suggest that experience and practice in other advanced economies will be ignored, but rather that the treatment will reflect European custom and attitudes as opposed to American, which have tended to dominate so much of the marketing literature.

Each volume is the work of an acknowledged authority on that subject and combines distillation of the best and most up-to-date research findings with a clear statement of their relevance to improved managerial practice. A concise style is followed throughout, and extensive use is made of summaries, checklists and references to related work. Thus each work may be viewed as both an introduction to and a reference work on its particular subject. Further, while each book is self-contained, the series as a whole comprises a handbook of marketing management.

The series is designed for both students and practitioners of marketing. Lecturers will find the treatment adequate as the foundation for in-depth study of each topic by more advanced students who have already pursued an introductory and broadly based course in marketing. Similarly, managers will find each book to be both a useful *aide-mémoire* and a reference source.

The titles so far published in the series are:

CONSUMER CHOICE

Gordon R. Foxall
Senior Lecturer in Marketing
Cranfield School of Management

© Gordon R. Foxall 1983

First published 1983 by
THE MACMILLAN PRESS LTD
London and Basingstoke
Companies and representatives throughout the world

ISBN 0 333 34226 7 (hard cover)
ISBN 0 333 34227 5 (paper cover)

Typeset in Great Britain by
MULTIPLEX MEDWAY LTD
Maidstone, Kent

Printed in Hong Kong

Contents

Preface

In an exploratory paper presented in 1976 to a conference of the Marketing Education Group (the leading representative body of British marketing academics), I suggested that consumer researchers were too ready to conceive of buyer behaviour as a function of 'the black box of the consumer's psyche' and argued that more attention should be given to situational, especially social, influences on consumer choice. At that time, my argument rested upon the observation that the former approach was producing few advances in the prediction of consumer behaviour compared with the effort it demanded. The small amount of research into the situational context of consumer choice which had been carried out seemed far more promising.

This book is also concerned with these themes. However the large amount of research material in both social psychology and marketing which has appeared in the past six years permits a more sophisticated and, I hope, convincing argument. It is intended as an introduction to wider reading for students and teachers of marketing at all levels, rather than as a conventional textbook of consumer behaviour. In particular, because one aim of the book is to encourage the critical re-evaluation of much that is familiar to consumer researchers and marketing educators, I have not used valuable space to provide detailed descriptions of what is readily found elsewhere. I have as a rule summarised the results and conclusions of others that are widely available in the expectation that interested readers will evaluate my interpretations by reference to the original sources.

I have found this a fascinating book to write. Although it is concerned with familiar themes, its recommendations for consumer research and marketing management are novel. Because of this I have welcomed the opportunities I have had to discuss its contents with social psychologists and marketing specialists. The presentation of a paper at a marketing theory seminar chaired by Professor Michael Baker resulted in valuable encouragement and guidance from the chairman and other participants, notably Malcolm Cunningham. Subsequently Professors R. P. Bagozzi, A. S. C. Ehrenberg and G. Goodhardt read and commented upon the paper and offered useful advice on how to proceed. At the University of Birmingham, I have benefited from the suggestions and advice of Dr David Booth, Reader in Psychology, and John Driver, Lecturer in Marketing. Linda Williamson typed the manuscript. I am grateful to them all for their assistance. Naturally, I take responsibility for the final version and offer my own attitudinal–behavioural inconsistency as a feeble explanation why I do not always heed their advice.

G.R.F.

Chapter 1
Introduction

The application of the behavioural sciences to the study of consumer choice has tended to be piecemeal. All too often concepts from sociology and social psychology have been sought for in order to 'explain' the observed phenomena only after the data have been collected. Progress has been haphazard. Even allowing that scientific advance is frequently the result of serendipity rather than planned, theory-grounded investigation, consumer research as both a commercially relevant activity and as the basis of a developing academic discipline is, more than should be the case, *ad hoc*.

Jacoby[1] refers to this as the 'atheoretic shotgun approach' of consumer researchers in which theory is ignored and the facts are allowed to 'speak for themselves'.[1] Although consumer researchers have managed to avoid some of the unproductive philosophical debates much beloved of some social scientists, they have often failed to make explicit the theoretical implications of the concepts and methods which they have borrowed from the parent disciplines. Such concepts and methods originate in a specific context and are defined and developed in terms of appropriate theories or paradigms which may be wholly inappropriate when they are transferred to novel analytical or explanatory frameworks.

If the theoretical background and meaning of borrowed concepts are ignored, it is hardly surprising that the development of the discipline is impeded. In the absence of recognition of the theoretical stance which is being adopted and of the critical evaluation which would derive from such awareness, alternative stances and radically different concepts are seldom sought or appreciated. As Brunsson says:

A characteristic of social science is the multitude of perspectives used by different researchers. The significant differences between research fields lie less in what is described than in how it is described. One important way of developing a social science is to apply new perspectives to a part of reality, thereby highlighting new features of the reality. Perspectives determine what data are seen, what theories are developed, and what kinds of results turn up.[2]

For all their eclecticism in the use of constructs and methods developed elsewhere, consumer researchers have tended to avoid any critical analysis of the perspectives in which those borrowed tools originated. They have thus curtailed their search for alternative perspectives. When the shortcomings of a given concept become apparent, the tendency is to attempt to make it more useful by refining analytical techniques (today quantitative, tomorrow qualitative) rather than seeking a more fruitful concept.

This is clearest in the case of consumer research's central concept, 'attitude'. The assumptions on which its use is based may be stated as follows: 'Behaviour is prefigured and largely determined by factors which exist (or can be hypothesised as existing) within the individual. Of all these intrapersonal elements, attitudes which consist of cognitions (beliefs), affect (emotion or feeling) and conation (action tendencies) are of pre-eminent importance in shaping behaviour to particular objects. The prediction of behaviour therefore depends upon obtaining accurate measurements of attitudes since behaviour will be consistent with the individual's underlying mental dispositions. Although attitudes are dynamic and may be modified as a result of behaviour, the key to changing behaviour consists in the modification of one or more components of attitudes, predominantly through the presentation of informative (or persuasive) messages.'

Any description of a complex perspective which is only four sentences long is naturally a simplification, but most consumer behaviour specialists would agree that the above description contains the major assumptions which underlie the use of the concept of attitude in marketing.

The response of consumer researchers to the inadequacies of a concept is exemplified by their reaction to the demonstrated inability of measures of attitude to predict behaviour consistently and reliably. New ideas, measures and methods of analysis abound but the usefulness of the concept for management hardly increases. Even when non-attitudinal variables such as situational influences are incorporated in the model, the fixation with attitudes as significant precursors of behaviour is so strong that it almost entirely precludes either a critical awareness of the prevailing perspective or a search for a radical alternative.

Only occasionally is even the need for a more innovative approach given formal recognition, partly because an awareness of this need requires a thorough appraisal of attitude research in marketing, an area whose scope is enormous. Mostyn has expressed such a need as a result of her own wide ranging review, 'Instead of trying to improve the A–B [attitudinal-behavioural] relationship with existing techniques or even trying to improve upon the techniques, it would be more meaningful if researchers could rethink the entire assumptive philosophy underlying the A–B relationship.'[3] She does not, however, express an opinion as to the nature of an alternative perspective. This book examines the proposition that an appropriate alternative might be akin to the following: 'Behaviour is the result, not of intrapersonal events, but of the consequences of previous behaviour in similar situations. The reward or reinforcement of that behaviour shapes and sustains present and future behaviour of the same or similar kind. Behaviour can thus be most effectively predicted from the pattern of reinforcements previously received by the individual and changing behaviour depends upon modifying the situation in which it occurs in such a way as to make the reward or reinforcement dependent on new responses.'

The evaluation of an alternative perspective or paradigm is a more painstaking activity than the mere recasting or existing descriptions of consumer behaviour in novel terminology. The rethinking suggested by Mostyn involves a thorough reassessment of the prevailing concepts, assumed relationships between them, and the ways in which they are made operational and measurable. It requires an assessment of the relevance of a new philosophy of human behaviour to consumer research, and rests ultimately on its capacity to make marketing management more effective.

This is an enormous task beyond the scope of a single book. What the following chapters will do therefore is examine more closely the prevailing paradigm within which consumer research is conducted and an alternative approach (Chapter 2), assess the usefulness of the key variable, attitude, which is derived from the current approach to consumer research and marketing management (Chapter 3), and point to some probable implications of a new perspective (Chapters 4 and 5). The purpose of the book is not to argue for the novel perspective – though its relative obscurity compared with the prevailing view requires that it be clearly and forcefully presented – but to explore its possibilities and to invite others to do the same.

Chapter 2

Paradigms of Choice

INTRODUCTION

Marketing, like engineering, medicine and law, did not begin as an academic subject or a body of knowledge taught and learned for its own sake. Rather, its origins are linked to the practical concerns of business management and, in particular, with the establishment of regular, formalised patterns of economic exchange in order to make possible higher material standards of living. In spite of great increases in the complexity of social and economic life, the aims of marketing management remain broadly similar. Indeed, while all of these disciplines are now institutionalised within the established frameworks of education and research, they can still be legitimately regarded as technologies, as well as areas of scholarship. They are technologies firmly based upon bodies of systematic or scientific knowledge and enquiry or are in the process of becoming so.

Business men and women usually avoid refering to the theories and academic disciplines which allegedly underpin their work and achievements. However it is highly probable that their success depends largely upon the accuracy of their beliefs about the nature of the economic and business relationships which are implicit in their activities. Keynes went as far as to say that, 'Practical men, who believe themselves to be quite exempt from intellectual influences, are usually the slaves of some defunct economist'.[1] Although this is an overstatement it is true that human behaviour, including marketing, is generally founded upon commonly held views about the salient components of social and economic situations, opinions about what can safely be ignored and the ways in which the individuals in these situations are likely to interact. Without such notions, consistent interaction with other members of society would be impossible as would the interventions in the physical world made possible by the various forms of technology.

Marketing management relies increasingly upon commonly held generalisations about the nature of consumer behaviour and the effect upon it of intervening in markets by means of the marketing mix. Recent progress in the introduction of marketing education to universities and colleges and its establishment as an integral part of management studies have hastened the systematic search for such generalisations. Special attention has been given to the exploration of consumers' decision making processes as manifested in the choice of particular brands and the rejection of others and in loyalty to specific retail outlets. The existence of consumer choice – or at least the inability of marketers to know in advance the selections made by customers – lies at the heart of marketing oriented management itself. High levels of competition among companies, accompanied by large amounts of discretionary income available to buyers, were the key structural factors in the development and adoption of the marketing concept as a contemporary business philosophy. This was because businessmen and women discovered that in order to achieve their own financial objectives they needed to fulfil the requirements of potential customers far more precisely than had previously been the case. And, ever since this discovery began to influence the actions of businessmen and women in the economic conditions of early twentieth century America, there has been a diversity of views about how marketing works, the extent to which marketers are able to analyse and understand consumers' wants and needs, and make use of their knowledge of consumers' psychological processes in order to persuade them to buy Brand *A* or to shop at the *X* Store.

In a volume of the *Library of Business Practice* concerned with advertising and published nearly three generations ago a perspective is found which is frequently encountered today to the effect that:

Advertising would be a simple proposition if the advertising man had ability to read the individual human mind. Unhappily – or perhaps happily – the advertising man has no supernatural power to scan a crowd and determine what each individual wants, or what argument would avail in a particular case . . . Here lies the art of advertising – to find the point of contact between the goods and the consumer. It is indeed an art that has had much to do with mindreading, not of individuals, but of classes. It is the art of knowing the weak spots of self-interest in any group of mankind – of knowing the psychological operation of advertising arguments.[2]

This quotation doubtless reflects the emerging sales orientation of the day. Its emphasis on advertising as a persuasive force rather than on integrated marketing is characteristic of a determination to sell rather than to market, an intent which is all too often met in the late twentieth century. Advertising and marketing are still seen in terms of persuading, of building the conviction which leads to purchases that favour a particular brand or store. But more significant is the continuing belief that marketing research must continue to probe the consumer's psyche in the hope that the mental processes which are the antecedents of choice will be discovered and, perhaps, made subject to managerial control.

A rather different emphasis, yet one which is built upon the same assumptions, occurs in another chapter of this volume and nicely illustrates the diversity of variations on the traditional and prevailing theme of consumer choice and marketing action:

> Underneath the changing forms of business stand the fixed motives of men. From the time of stone axes, when men bartered necessities one for the other, the reasons behind the bargaining have always been the same. The man who knows how to sell or advertise today does not need to invent novel arguments or create new demands. Instead, he builds his appeal upon the foundation motives of hunger, cold, self-preservation, pride, love, enjoyment, gain. The man who plumbs the spirit and attitude of the buyer, who frames the right appeal in kind and aim, succeeds whether he does business by stage coach or limited train. The problem, then, is: can these various appeals – these vital motives of the buying public – be analysed and charted? Keen businessmen have demonstrated the answer beyond doubt or question. They have been and can be so charted and so used every day.[3]

The widespread view of the role of marketing, then as now, was based upon the belief that human choice is the outcome of mental deliberation or cognitive processes and that persuasion consists of the influencing or manipulation of those internal events. The purpose of this book is to demonstrate that there is an alternative viable framework within which consumer choice may be conceptualised and analysed. This approach is not entirely new to marketing but has received far less attention than that which stresses the need to delve profoundly into consumers' cognitive processes. In contrast to that idea, the alternative framework focuses upon the behaviour of consumers in itself and the environment within which it takes place. In the terminology of modern psychology, the book is concerned with the extent to which the individual consumer's 'locus of control' lies within his physical body, brain or mind, or is external to the individual.

Although this book draws upon the literature of psychology to a greater degree than is usual in marketing and necessarily makes much use of the terminology of that discipline, it is intended to contribute to the principles and practice of marketing management. The acceptance of one of the sets of assumptions discussed in this and the following chapters strongly influences the direction and content of consumer research programmes and the ways in which marketing managers intervene in markets. Far from being a psychological treatise, then, this book is an attempt to convey to the student and practitioner of marketing the fascination of progress in consumer research as it increasingly provides a scientific basis to marketing technology. The title of this chapter refers to the two central themes upon which the argument of the whole book rests and it is appropriate to review their meanings before returning to the subject of consumer choice.

CONCEPTS OF CHOICE

The definition of choice appears initially to be a straightforward, commonsense task. Hansen states that:

> We all intuitively understand what a choice is. It is classically illustrated by the person walking down a road who hesitates at a fork in the road before choosing which route to take. We all agree that he is faced with a choice. If, however, the example is changed slightly, it is more doubtful whether we are still talking about a choice. The person walking on a sidewalk, when confronted with a puddle, changes his direction slightly and continues. In this case, few people would say that a choice is involved.[4]

Hansen distinguishes choice from other forms of behaviour by pointing out that it involves a multiplicity of possible outcomes, the arousal of conflict as a result of the individual's perception that mutually exclusive outcomes are open to him, and an attempt to reduce this conflict by means of cognitive activity. Thus when an individual is faced with the selection of a single course of action from among several ostensible options:

> a particular pattern of reactions can be observed: hesitation, inspection of alternatives, uncertainty . . . [C]onscious and unconscious brain processes occur, processes that may possibly be observed directly and are reflected in measurements such as electrocardiograms and galvanic skin response. These suggest that a conflict is present and that cognitive activities occur.[5]

It is perhaps true that few laymen would disagree with the proposition that the first example given by Hansen involves choice while the second does not and, as the word 'choice' is employed in everyday discourse, the distinction is clear enough. But scientists and philosophers have developed systems of thought which do not distinguish between these two examples. Sartre would argue, for instance, that the individual confronted with the puddle did have a choice and that it is 'bad faith' to claim that he could not have stepped into the water had he so decided.[6] More relevant to the framework of conceptualisation and analysis advanced in the present work is the proposition that the person in the first example had as little freedom of choice as the one in the second: both, on the basis of previous identical or similar experience and the consequences of previous behaviour in similar situations, would be capable of only one course of action, that which was taken. In the words of B. F. Skinner, the psychologist most frequently associated with this framework, 'To exercise choice is simply to act, and the choice a person is capable of making is the act itself. The person requires freedom to make it simply in the sense that he can make it only if there are no restraints – either in the physical situation or in other conditions affecting his behaviour.'[7] The first explanation, that of the individual faced with a puddle, places the locus of control entirely within the individual; the second, that which focuses on the act itself as the only 'choice' available, places the locus of control firmly outside the person.

PARADIGMS AND PROGRESS

The differences between these accounts stem largely from the different frameworks of conceptualisation and analysis which investigators bring to the study of their subject matter. During the last two decades, appreciation of the role of such frameworks in scientific progress has increased substantially in a wide range of fields of research. This development has followed the publication by Kuhn of the view that scientific development advances more significantly as a result of the revolutionary substitution of an innovatory framework or paradigm for the existing framework than by the evolutionary accumulation of knowledge.[8] The idea of paradigmatic scientific progress is rather more complicated than this but the following brief account cannot be improved upon as a concise description of what is involved in Kuhn's thesis. Social psychologists, Jones and Gerard refer to a paradigm as:

> essentially a model for asking research questions. Paradigms are partly a matter of broad theoretical outlook or perspective, partly a matter of preferred methods of obtaining evidence, and partly a matter of the standard by which such evidence is to be evaluated. In the developmental history of a particular discipline, a certain paradigm may characterise the outlook of one or more generations of scientists. Eventually, certain anomalous findings may force a shift to a new paradigm, bringing about radical changes in perspective, new suggestions about where to look for evidence, and new standards of evaluation. The change from Aristotelian to Galilean physics represents a very broad paradigm shift. The shift from Newtonian mechanics to Einsteinian relativity provides a more recent example. The point is that these shifts are more than changes in theories appropriate to account for a particular set of phenomena. They are shifts that revolutionise our entire scientific stance and radically change the way in which investigators view their subject matter.[9]

In contrast to the popular view that scientific progress is the straightforward result of the continual accumulation of facts within a given framework of conception and analysis, Kuhn hypothesises that 'mature' sciences, notably physics, develop by means of dramatic paradigmatic supersession. The revolutionary replacement of a previously productive paradigm has profound implications for the concepts that are deemed relevant, the canons of theoretical judgement which are applicable and the appropriate practical methods of data collection, techniques of analysis and procedures of interpretation. Such a revolution appears to be a periodic necessity of advance.

How do these revolutions occur? Because of the essentially ideological nature of scientific paradigms, they are not themselves amenable to direct empirical test. A paradigm consists, after all, of the most general, albeit highly influential, beliefs of a scientific community with respect to the investigation of reality. Kuhn defines a paradigm as, 'what the members of a scientific community share . . . some implicit body of intertwined theoretical and methodological belief that permits selection, evaluation and criticism'.[10] This is closely akin to what Thelen and Withal nominate a 'frame of reference' by which the researcher, 'perceives and interprets events by means of a conceptual structure of generalisations or contexts, postulates about what is essential, assumptions as to what is valuable, attitudes about what is possible, and ideas about what will work effectively'.[11] Paradigmatic transition can be a slow process: Einstein's seminal papers were largely ignored by scientists for some fifteen years before their acceptance began to displace Newtonian physics. Experimental testing of some of the propositions derived from the Einsteinian paradigm has become possible only as science has developed the space age. More fundamental to Kuhn's thesis than this, however, is the observation that such is the nature of paradigm based 'normal' science that its exponents act very conservatively, rejecting initially any subversive philosophy which threatens the tenets of the paradigm within which they are working. The first cracks in the scientific community's acceptance of the prevailing paradigm appear only as a result of the clear inability of theories devised within it to account for new findings. Repeated theoretical failure often results in a scientific crisis, the proliferation of theories to account for the new evidence. The crisis ends with the general acceptance of a novel paradigm that accommodates both those new theories which are deemed valid and those elements of the older body of knowledge which are held to be worthy of retention. Thus while paradigms cannot be subjected to direct testing as can hypotheses, they give rise to the theories, models and hypotheses whose empirical verification or refutation eventually confirm or disconfirm the prevailing conventional wisdom.

Kuhn's hypothesis was developed in the course of his studies of historical developments in the physical sciences. The social sciences may well prove to be an exception to the pattern of progress he identified. In the physical sciences, for example, a single paradigm usually dominates the entire scientific community most of the time. Multiple paradigms and the division of the scientific community along fundamental lines occurs, by and large, only during critical phases of development. This is manifestly not the case in the social sciences where a plurality of competing paradigms is usually apparent. The possibility of paradigmatic supersession is a constant fact of life for the social scientist, even though it is unlikely that displaced frames of reference ever completely disappear. Within recent years, for example, there has been renewed effort directed towards the promotion of 'Austrian economics' which presents a radical alternative to the generally accepted neoclassical/Keynesian amalgam, quite distinct ideas of the ways in which markets work, novel methodological imperatives and different implications for government policy.[12] In sociology, to take a second example, there has been since the mid 1960s a re-emphasis on radically phenomenological methods of investigation.[13] Neither of these paradigms is entirely new; nor is their acceptance likely to be total.

Social science disciplines are usually characterised by the simultaneous flourishing of more than one paradigm and drawn out debates between their exponents rather than by conformity to a single, general philosophy of the nature of the discipline. Consequently when change does occur it is usually less dramatic and less obviously revolutionary than in the mature sciences. That the social sciences do not correspond precisely to Kuhn's model of scientific progress ought not, however, to obscure the value of conceiving of the development of these disciplines in terms derived from it. Psychology – and the study of consumer behaviour conceived in psychological terms – contains two broad meta-theoretical stances, two broad paradigms: that which casts behaviour as the result of intrapersonal, cognitive information processing, which explains choice as the outcome of deliberation and decision making; and that which interprets behaviour in terms of the consequences of previous behaviour, which describes choice in terms of determined responses to environmental (and, less significantly in the present context, inherited) stimuli. The description and analysis of consumer behaviour in ways which are commercially and academically valid and reliable require a more detailed understanding of these paradigmatic stances.

COGNITIVE INFORMATION PROCESSING

The popular view of psychology as the formal study of mind, mental phenomena and processes, or of internal, subjective or covert experience was, until recently, not shared by the majority of psychologists. From the early years of this century until the mid to late 1950s, most psychologists adhered to the belief propounded by Watson, 'the father of behaviourism', that so-called mental phenomena were beyond the scope of a science of behaviour.[14] During those years, the behaviourist framework of analysis characterised the 'normal science' of psychology and, although there was some work done outside of this paradigm throughout the period, the shift which enthroned cognitive psychology as the prevailing conventional wisdom is a fairly recent occurrence. Members of a symposium convened to identify and discuss contemporary issues in cognitive psychology, the proceedings of which were published in 1973, clearly understood the emergence (or re-emergence) of the cognitive paradigm in terms of Kuhn's ideas of the nature of scientific progress.[15]

That cognitive phenomena provide the basis of psychology's prevailing paradigm is evident from the observation that, while psychologists increasingly recognise situational and other external environmental factors as influences upon behaviour, their definitions of psychology and, especially significant, the way they demarcate it from other social, behavioural and physiological sciences are expressed predominantly in terms of perception, memory, thought and emotions. This is also evident from the stress they place upon the mediating roles of cognitive factors even when tracing, analysing and interpreting the effects of extrapersonal influences on behaviour. In an address to the American Psychological Association, which was also presented in 1973, Hebb asked 'what is psychology about?' and answered that, 'Psychology is about the mind: the central issue, the great mystery, the toughest problem of all . . .'[16] He went on to define mind as 'the capacity for thought' and thought as 'the integrative activity of the brain – that activity up in the control tower that, during waking hours, overrides reflex response and frees behaviour from sense dominance.'[17]

The peculiar focus of the social psychologist has been stated by Tajfel and Fraser as consisting in his interest, 'in information about how the various social structures, social systems or groups affect an individual's way of viewing the world in which he lives and of acting in it; and about how his "nature", i.e. his motives, perceptions and interpretations will in turn affect his functioning in groups and the relationships between groups'.[18] Thus, while the social psychologist shares the field of intergroup relations with numerous other professional investigators his focus consists uniquely:

in establishing links between an individual's interpretation or perception of social situations and his behaviour and attitudes towards the groups to which he belongs and other groups; in the
ways in which various kinds of intergroup situations may affect an
individual's motives . . . and in the ways in which certain motives
may affect, in turn, the nature of these intergroup relations; in
analysing the process of communication which help or hinder the
diffusion of certain modes of behaviour and attitudes towards in-
groups and outgroups.[19]

The essential theme of psychological study is, according to this, the
prevailing perspective, not only individual and group behaviour of itself but the mental antecedents which are assumed to determine it.

In spite of the somewhat pejorative label attached to this perspective, the description of cognitive psychology offered by Moore summarises well its dominant character.

Mentalism may be considered as a particular orientation to the
explanation of behaviour, involving the following implicit or
explicit features: (a) the bifurcation of human experience into a behavioural and a pre-behavioural dimension (b) the use of
psychological terms to refer to organo-centric entities from the pre-
behavioural dimension, and (c) the use of organo-centric entities
as causally effective antecedents in explaining behaviour.[20]

Intervening Variables

Some of the earliest challenges to the rigid stimulus–response
paradigm (which approached behaviour solely in terms of the
physical stimuli, S, such as heat and light, which act upon a subject,
and the response, R, in terms of movement elicited) originated in
the work of behaviourists. For example, an interesting expression
of the view that behaviour can be accurately understood, predicted
and controlled only when intrapersonal mediating processes are considered occurs in the writings of Tolman.[21] Not content to study
behaviour exclusively in terms of S–R mechanisms, Tolman hypothesised 'intervening variables' which summarised the effects on behaviour of previous experience or learning and inherited influences;
these mediating factors were assumed to modify the effects of stimuli
in individual cases, accounting for variations in response. Tolman's

central interests remained in the sphere of investigations of the relationships between stimuli and the responses they evoke and he attributed his work to the behaviourist paradigm since he ascribed the intrapersonal variables upon which his theories depended to reflex, physiological factors rather than mental events.[22] His work had a profound influence upon other behaviourists[23] but in paradigmatic terms it encouraged the progress of cognitive psychology since many subsequent researchers comprehended the organo-centric intervening variables as psychological or mental processes.

The growth of Gestalt psychology,[24] which influenced Tolman through the tenet that intervening factors constituted the psychological pattern through which stimuli received subjective meaning, also facilitated the diffusion of the nonbehaviourist paradigm. Such variables as beliefs, attitudes, personality traits, motives and values were assumed to mediate stimuli and responses by psychologists who adopted the stimulus $\rightarrow$ organism $\rightarrow$ response or $S \rightarrow [0] \rightarrow R$ model. Within this perspective, the classification and measurement of stimuli and responses allow inferences to be drawn with respect to the nature of the 'black box' of internal, psychological processes which are not available for direct investigation.

Adherents of this viewpoint differ in that some make the assumption that the inferred processes correspond in some way to actual inner states while others argue that the posited intervening variables are of an entirely hypothetical character.[25] The operative point is, however, that intra-organismic variables now play a crucial role in the explanation of overt action which is no longer understood to be the simple result of stimulus inputs and conditioned reflexes. Indeed, once the intervening variables are taken to correspond to actual or hypothetical mental processes, it is natural to enquire further into the nature and properties of these processes. Their capacity to act upon and transform informational inputs has become a preoccupation of social psychologists. Thus Newcomb, Turner and Converse assert that 'Man's most distinctive physiological equipment is the mind itself – an unparalleled tool for processing and storing great quantities of information. The complexity of his behaviour is dependent not only on his capacity to retain much information in his memory, but also on the fact that this stored information is organised in useful ways.'[26] In these two sentences they summarise succinctly the rationale of cognitive psychology.

Cognitive Psychology

The contemporary psychological study of cognitive information processing is, however, immensely more sophisticated than either the basic $S \rightarrow [0] \rightarrow R$ model or any short quotation can convey. Cognitive psychology tends to de-emphasise the role of the environment as a source of stimuli of behaviour. Whilst not denying the environment as the inevitable source of external stimuli, cognitive psychologists place more stress on and devote a greater proportion of their effort to the investigation of internal stimuli, i.e. those intrapersonal, mental events and processes which are consequent upon environmental inputs, through which the recipient individual's experience is constructed and by which contingent responses are initiated.[27] Neisser illustrates this general proposition in the statement that the study of visual cognition, 'deals with the process by which a perceived, remembered and thought-about world is brought into being from as unpromising a beginning as the retinal patterns'.[28] The investigation of cognition is not, of course, confined to the consequences of visual stimulation but:

> refers to all the processes by which the sensory input is transformed, reduced, elaborated, stored, recovered, and used. It is concerned with these processes even when they operate in the absence of relevant stimulation, as in images and hallucinations. Such terms as *sensation, perception, imagery, retention, recall, problem-solving,* and *thinking*, among many others, refer to hypothetical stages or aspects of cognition.[29]

Specifically, cognitive psychology focuses upon the reception by the organism of inputs which take the form of stimuli having their origin in the environment.[30] The capacity of organisms to recognise information via the senses is generally greater than their capacity to process internalised information effectively. Consequently this process of reception avoids sensory overload by incorporating a highly selective form of attention. Some of the information which impinges upon the individual's sensory registers nevertheless passes through the attentive and perceptual filters by which cognitive overload is avoided, into short term (or temporary, working) memory which interacts with the long term memory (or permanent memory store). (See Figure 1.1.) All of these activities involve cognitive processes which place the environmental inputs into the context of the individual's remembered and recalled experience, motives, goals, and other constructs which

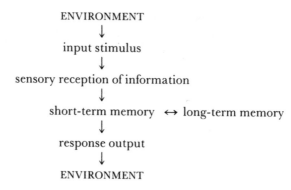

Figure 1.1 *Cognitive information processing in the individual*

facilitate the comprehension, interpretation and positioning of the novel stimulus. The endpoint of the stimulus induced information processing is a 'response output' which often takes the form of verbal or overt behaviour.

Atkinson and Shiffrin attach pivotal significance within the entire cognitive process to the role of temporary, working memory 'because the processes carried out in the short-term store are under the immediate control of the subject and govern the flow of information in the memory system; they can be called into play at the subject's discretion, with enormous consequences for performance.'[31] Short term memory holds the key to the control of the entire information processing sequence precisely because it mediates, co-ordinates and integrates immediate environmental inputs with the permanent memory store which encapsulates past experience in subjective form. Short term memory processes carry out these functions while editing and giving a subjective meaning to the information received by the sensory registers so that subsequent processing or use of the data can take place. Short term memory shapes cognitive, information processing in the individual and, thereby, his or her output responses through such operations as rehearsal (the repetition of information until it can be recalled at will or written down for more permanent storage), coding (linking the novel informatin with other, retrievable data), imaging (storage of verbal information in visual form) and decision and retrieval strategy making. Short term memory thus has particular implications for exposure to new information, the precise operation of selective attention and perception, forgetting and the modification and effect of attitudes and behavioural intentions.

The parallel between the human cognitive transformation of information and the information processing functions of computers has frequently been drawn.[32] However, the early enthusiasms of advocates of the view that digital computers *simulated* human information processing has given way to the idea that computer *programming* is analogous to the way in which the human mind or brain operates. The simulation concept ignores the limitations of computers to represent human mental processes. For example computers lack the capacity to be distracted or emotional. The requisite role of the cognitive psychologist is therefore 'analogous to that of a man trying to discover how a computer has been programmed'.[33] Neither is concerned more than superficially with the composition of the entity controlled by the information processing in question (the nature of the physical computing machinery or the physiology of the living organism) but each is vitally interested in unravelling the procedural rules and routines which govern the information processing itself. There is always the danger, well recognised by cognitivists, of employing the analogy of computer programming too rigidly and thereby presenting as crude a view of 'man the machine' as the crudest forms of behaviourism. What distinguishes the psychology of cognitive information processing from the more mechanistic approaches of the behaviourists is, according to Bower, the assumption by the former that the ego or self acts as an 'executive monitor' which can intervene in the situations in which human problems arise in order to permit the selection of appropriate responses from the available options: the self thus acts as 'an overseer or monitor controlling mental processes'.[24]

Information Processing in Consumer Research

The fundamental tenets of the cognitive information processing paradigm have pervaded textbooks of consumer behaviour ever since they first appeared in the late 1960s. Such concepts as perception, cognition, learning, memory, personality, belief, attitudes, and purchase intentions have served well the attempt to describe and explain consumers' prebehavioural 'decision processes' and their behavioural outcomes. Like the business writers of the early twentieth century quoted earlier, modern prescriptive accounts of consumer research and marketing management (particularly those concerned with the administration of marketing communications and the evaluation of the effects of advertising) emphasise strongly the need to identify and measure consumers' prepurchase cognitive processes.[35] These prescriptions rest upon the argument that in effective persuasion the buyer's prepurchase processing of information, gained significantly though not exclusively through advertising, strengthens or modifies his attitudes and purchase intentions which in turn maintain or cause changes in his buying behaviour, particularly with respect to brand choice. Studies of the 'communications process' and its elements – *the message source* (analysed in such terms as credibility, likeability and status), *the message* (ordering of arguments, one sided and two sided appeals, and message contents) and *the audience* (persuasibility, self esteem, attitudinal position), such as those conducted by Hovland and Janis in the classic Yale University Communications Research Programme,[36] are expected to lead to its control.

This approach figures strongly in the widely known marketing models of consumer behaviour. All of these models are based on the computer flow chart logical sequence and all espouse the view that prepurchase mental events and processes, notably 'attitudes', are proximally causative of consumer choice behaviour and that behavioural change is a function of the antecedent modification of attitudes.

One of the earliest comprehensive models of consumer choice, that published by Andreasen in 1965, attaches paramount significance to the influence of attitudes on purchase outcomes.[37] Andreasen postulates that information which passes through the consumer's 'filter' (that is, screening criteria which may be described in terms of perceptual selectivity and attitudes towards the information source) impacts upon the potential customer's attitude (which is conceived as a tricomponential structure consisting of cognitive, affective and conative interactions). Attitude formation, which is influenced by personal, psychological and environmental factors as well as the processing of novel information, is followed by (i) immediate product/brand choice or (ii) attenuated information seeking or (iii) no action. Such constraints as the availability of purchasing power, the precedence of other purchase requirements and physical capacity determine the timing of the selected item's purchase. Finally, ownership, consumption and experiential feedback to the consumer's internal 'information store' (presumably long term memory) complete each repetition of the decision making sequence.

Nicosia portrays the impact of a persuasive marketing communication for an extremely discontinuous innovation upon the consumer who is expected to 'internalise' its message.[38] If internalisation – which is dependent upon the continuity of the perceptual, environmental and cognitive fields which facilitate or impede the acceptance of the message – occurs, the result is the formation of an *attitude* towards the radically new item. *Motivation*, which is the assumed outcome of subsequent search behaviour, determines, subject to brand availability, in-store advertising and price acceptability, the purchase response. Further attitude formation is assumed to depend less on advertising than did the initial purchase since repetitive decision processes rely to some extent upon the results of experience gained by prior purchase and consumption. Consumers' *dispositions* are, nonetheless, regarded as crucial determinants of repeat buying patterns.

Howard and Sheth similarly describe the buyer's 'response sequence' (attention → brand comprehension → attitude → intention → purchase) in terms of the cognition, affect and conation which are the result of 'symbolic communication'.[39] The mental *ambiguity* arising from a marketing or social stimulus leads to the search for, and processing of information, a procedure which terminates in the formation of an *attitude* towards the product or brand on offer and the consequent establishment of a buying *intention* which causes purchase. Of all the comprehensive models of consumer decision making, that of Howard and Sheth makes the most explicit use of the $S → [O] → R$ model (see, in particular, Chapter 9, which deals with symbolic communication). Engel, Blackwell and Kollat advance a broadly similar model in which perceived information leads, via memory, to problem recognition, search, and the evaluation of alternatives, in a process which consists of the familiar belief → attitude → intentions sequence and, ultimately, choice.[40] Their textbook presents an account of consumer decision making which has been painstakingly constructed through the careful integration of concepts and relationships derived from contemporary cognitive psychology: memory, selective sensory and perceptual reactions to exposure to informational stimuli, the interpretation of the meanings of stimuli, reception of the message through its comprehension and acceptance, and cognitive response as the partially processed information is admitted to long term memory.

'Hierarchies of Effects'

In addition to these comprehensive models of consumer choice behaviour, there have developed over the last seven decades a range of 'hierarchy of effects' models. These models vary considerably in their sophistication but they all suggest an essentially similar prepurchase process comprising a sequence of psychological states of increasing comprehension and desire and culminating in the 'strong conviction' which determines purchase and its outcome. A selection of these models of consumer information processing is shown in Table 2.1 which also presents outline summaries of some of the models which have been described.

Table 2.1 *Information processing depictions of consumer choice*

Author(s)	Year	Sequence
Starch	1923	Seeing→ Reading→ Believing→ Remembering→ Acting
Strong	1925	Awareness→ Interest→ Desire→ Action
Lionberger Rogers	1960 } 1962 }	Awareness→ Interest→ Evaluation→ Trial→ Adoption
Colley	1961	Unawareness→ Awareness→ Comprehension→ Conviction→ Action
Lavidge and Steiner	1961	Awareness→ Knowledge→ Liking→ Preference→ Conviction→ Purchase (i.e., cognition→ affect→ conation)
McGuire	1969	Exposure→ Attention→ Comprehension→ Yielding→ Retention→ Behaviour
Howard and Sheth	1969	Attention→ Brand Comprehension→ Attitude→ Intention→ Purchase
Rogers and Shoemaker	1971	Knowledge→ Persuasion→ Decision → Confirmation
McGuire	1976	Exposure→ Perception→ Comprehension→ Agreement→ Retention→ Retrieval→ Decision making→ Action
Engel, Blackwell and Kollat	1978	Perceived information→ Problem recognition→ Search→ Evaluation of Alternatives→ Beliefs→ Attitudes→ Intentions→ Choice
Britt	1978	Exposing→ Attending→ Perceiving → Learning and Remembering→ Motivating→ Persuading→ Desired Action

Sources overleaf

Sources: D. Starch, *Principles of Advertising* (New York: A. W. Shaw, 1923); U. K. Strong, *Principles of Selling* (New York: McGraw-Hill, 1925); H. F. Lionberger, *Adoption of New Ideas and Practices* (Ames, Iowa: State Univesity Press, 1960); E. M. Rogers, *Diffusion of Innovation* (New York: Free Press, 1962); R. H. Colley, *Defining Advertising Goals for Measured Results* (Association of National Advertisers, 1961); R. J. Lavidge and G. A. Steiner, 'A Model for Predictive Measurement of Advertising Effectiveness', *Journal of Marketing*, vol. 25, no. 4 (1961) pp. 59–62; W. J. McGuire, 'An Information-Processing Model of Advertising Effectiveness', *Symposium on Behaviour and Management Science in Marketing* (Chicago, Illinois: Chicago University, 1969), also in Davis and Silk (eds), *Behavioural and Marketing Science in Marketing* (New York: Wiley, 1978) pp. 156–80; J. Howard and J. N. Sheth, *The Theory of Buyer Behaviour* (New York: Wiley, 1969); E.M. Rogers and F. F. Shoemaker, *Communication of Innovations* (New York: Free Press, 1971); W. J. McGuire, 'Some Internal Psychological Factors Influencing Consumer Choice', *Journal of Consumer Research*, vol. 2, no. 4 (1976) pp. 302–19. Cf. K. S. Palda, 'The Hypothesis of a Hierarchy of Effects: A Partial Evaluation', *Journal of Marketing Research*, vol. 3, no. 1 (1966), pp. 13–24; J. F. Engel, R. D. Blackwell and D. T. Kollat, *Consumer Behaviour*, 3rd edn (Hindsdale, Illinois: Dryden, 1978); S. H. Britt, *Psychological Principles of Marketing and Consumer Behaviour* (Lexington, Mass.: D. C. Heath, 1978).

Examples of the manner in which the general cognitive information processing model of consumer choice has been incorporated into the marketing literature are so widely available as to require no corresponding, detailed exposition here. (The interested reader should examine the comprehensive exposition presented by Engel, Blackwell and Kollat or the more concise paper by McGuire.)[41] Table 2.2 sets out the scheme which is typically assumed, along with the major related research issues and managerial concerns. Briefly the assumed pattern of cognitive processing follows the scheme employed in mainstream psychology with the added emphasis of certain managerially relevant components of the overall process. The contribution of attitudes to behavioural (purchase) intentions and the assumption that behavioural intentions correlate highly with manifest behavioural choice looms especially large in the marketing based study and depiction of consumer behaviour. The information processing approaches of Howard and Sheth and of Engel, Blackwell and Kollat draw particular attention to the attitude → intention → purchase sequence although it is taken for granted throughout the consumer behaviour literature.

An additional component of the prevailing paradigm of both cognitive psychology and consumer research is the assignment to individuals of a framework of motivation which adds a dynamic aspect to the behaviour under investigation. So important has the psychology of motivation become, especially in the wake of the psychoanalytical revolution, that dynamic psychology could well be considered here a third paradigm were it not so well integrated in consumer research with the information processing perspective. Once again, the points of contact between dynamic psychology and consumer research – from Maslow's 'hierarchy of needs' to Freudian suppression and repression and beyond – are well covered in consumer behaviour texts[42] and there is no need for elaboration here.

The managerial implications of the argument advanced in this book form part of a later chapter but it is worth noting briefly the consequences of cognitive information processing for the conception of marketing's requisite response to consumer behaviour. Ehrenberg and Goodhardt present the general implications of cognitively based models in terms of marketing communications.[43] In doing this they provide a useful summary of the conclusions of an information processing analysis for the use by marketing managers of the entire marketing mix as a persuasive device by marketing managers. These authors use the phrase 'the strong theory of advertising' to identify that view of marketing communications which depicts it as very persuasive, moving the customer along a 'hierarchy of effects' sequence until his or her *conviction* of the merits of a given brand and consequent *desire* to own and use it compel the appropriate purchase and sustained brand loyalty. Thus the consumer information processing perspective accords well with the predominant idea of the use of advertising in marketing and, indeed, the persuasive use of the entire marketing mix by attributing to marketing considerable power to determine purchase and consumption behaviour via the influence of prebehavioural mental processes.

Texts on consumer behaviour, marketing management and advertising typically advocate this approach in order to ensure managerial manipulation of those aspects of the source – message – audience continuum which are believed to be within their control.[44] In particular, in modern accounts of the contributions of consumer research to managerial decision making, consumers' attitudes and the purchase intentions derived from them take precedence over other mental constructs and, on occasion, subsume the effects of social and environmental stimuli. Since attitudes are cast in this approach as the primal causative antecedents of behaviour, the primary task of consumer research is held to be the identification and validation of more sensitive and powerful means of defining and measuring them.[45] The effect of this approach on marketing research and managerial planning has been immense: from the 'perceptual mapping' which underpins

Table 2.2 *Cognitive information processing as a consumer research paradigm*

Process components	Typical research issues	Typical managerial concerns
Attention	Arousal, interest, exposure patterns, sensory reception, social and personality contexts, avoidance of discrepant information, information search pre-attentive delay, attentive screening.	Segmentation of markets, media selection, use of fear or humour, packaging, sensory stimuli.
Perception	Perceptual selectivity, sensory overload and filtering of information, post attentive delay, perceptual shift, stimulus intensity, reinforcement history, needs states, values, expectation, perception by exception.	Dimensional factors, packaging size and shape, repetition, stimulus intensity, sensory stimulation.
Comprehension	Short term memory, interpretation and meaning, abstraction, verbal and visual encoding rehearsal, initial processing of information.	Use of linguistic and visual explanation, stimulation of information seeking; repetition of message.
Acceptance	Agreement, persuasion, attitude change, personal and social characteristics, message discrepancy, credulity, receptivity to emotional appeals, attribution of motives.	Source credibility, media selection and copywriting, structure of appeals (one sided/two sided appeals), proximity and recency, emotional appeals, reference groups.

Table 2.2 *continued*

Process components	Typical research issues	Typical managerial concerns
Information storage and retrieval	Retention, memory and memory decay, forgetting, recall, retrieval, decoding, temporal effects, delayed processing, personal and social influences or remembering and forgetting, short term and long term memory interactions, information search.	Evocative advertising, emotional appeals (e.g. to nostalgia), provision of information, stimulation to information seeking, stimulation of interpersonal communication.
Establishment of preferences	Choice strategies, decision making processes, risk and uncertainty, elimination of options, evaluation, use of information, evaluative criteria, goals and expectations.	Comparative advertising, reinforcement, point of sale communication, sales promotions.
Behaviour	Attitudinal-behavioural consistency, behavioural intentions and their correlation with behaviour and its outcomes, unconscious motivation, dissonance reduction, purchase and consumption.	Manipulation of purchase and consumption situations, product availability, pricing, repeat buying, reduction of postdecisional dissonance.

brand 'positioning' to the measurement of consumers' sensitivity to price, from the measurement of store 'images' to the motivation of consumers to ascend a hierarchy of behavioural effects, the academic and professional marketing literatures are replete with synonyms for 'attitude' and 'attitudinal change'. Marketing managers and commercial consumer researchers, as well as marketing academics, evince strong acceptance of the relationship between attitudes and behaviour posited by cognitive psychology and of the derivative argument that behavioural change necessarily requires antecedent attitudinal change induced primarily by persuasive marketing communications, notably advertising.[46]

BEHAVIOURISM

In place of the comprehensive hierarchy of effects models of consumer behaviour, Ehrenberg and Goodhardt present a model which is consistent with a 'weak theory of advertising' in which marketing communications work primarily through suggestion and reinforcement.[47] The descriptive model of consumer choice which they advocate is based upon a three-stage sequence of buying: awareness → trial → reinforcement (or ATR). Advertising which is aimed at establishing awareness of a new product or brand often relies upon obtrusive effects and repetition in order to overcome the discrimination (or, in the terminology of cognitive psychology, the perceptual selectivity) by which consumers avoid messages concerned with unknown or currently unused brands. Awareness is, nevertheless, created or rekindled by advertising only with difficulty: there are no strongly persuasive marketing techniques even at this inaugural phase of the consumer choice sequence. Some consumers who nevertheless notice such advertising try the brand, albeit in an atmosphere of ignorance and uncertainty, for no amount of informative advertising or interpersonal communication can provide the experiential knowledge which only a product trial can supply.

The key role of advertising in this scheme is the reinforcement of whatever satisfaction the customer feels as a result of buying and using the product. It is not, however, the sole source of reinforcement: word of mouth communication and the purchaser's direct, comparative observation also fulfil this role. If continued purchase of the brand results from this reinforcement, advertising continues to perform the function of reminding the consumer of the benefits of the brand in question.

The primary role of competitive brand advertising, according to Ehrenberg and Goodhardt, is not to increase market share (there is no evidence of the sales effectiveness of advertising for established brands) but to prevent the erosion of sales levels. In other words, advertising such brands is indicative of a defensive strategy, 'advertising helps to keep one's satisfied customers by reinforcing their existing habits and attitudes. It is the price to pay for staying in the market.'[48]

The ATR model applies to frequently and infrequently purchased products, new and established brands, and brands with stable sales levels as well as those with dynamic sales trends. Its importance in the present argument, however, stems from its emphasis on behaviour (and behavioural change) preceding attitude formation (and attitudinal change). Only after a brand has been purchased and used can conviction and strong desire (to retain the cognitive terminology a little longer) be built and these are the result first and foremost of direct favourable experience with the item, in the absence of which, no amount of 'persuasive' advertising will induce the repeat purchasing upon which brand marketing strategies are heavily dependent. In place of the depiction of behavioural change as a function of prior attitudinal change which in turn derives from internal information processing prior to purchase, the proposed sequence is now (i) brand trial, stimulated by the reception and acceptance of some modicum of information but, of necessity, an experiment which occurs in a state of great uncertainty, followed by (ii) the reinforcement of the purchase, partly through advertising and social communication but primarily as a consequence of the user's evaluation of the merits of purchase and consumption outcomes.

The conclusions of this train of argument, though they are not necessarily all of the processes postulated by the ATR model, are consistent with a paradigm which provides an alternative framework of analysis to that of cognitive information processing and different managerial prescriptions from those hitherto discussed. This is the behaviour modification perspective, the application of which to marketing has been the subject of recent papers by Nord and Peter and Rothschild and Gaidis.[49] Behavioural learning theory is by no means unknown in marketing and has had a distinct influence on several cognate fields of research. Members of the Yale communications research team, to which reference has been made, derived assumptions and hypotheses from such learning theorists as Hull and Doob. Fishbein and Ajzen acknowledge similar influences on their own work, which has had some impact upon consumer research.[50] Nevertheless, the advocacy of a behaviourist paradigm as a means of guiding general marketing and consumer research is innovatory. Although the perspective proposed by Nord and Peter, and Rothschild and Gaidis owes more to the social learning approaches of Staats and Bandura[51] the most prolific philosopher of behaviourism is Skinner and, although his proposals are more radical than those thus far advanced by marketing specialists, consideration of his work provides the most appropriate introduction to behaviourist principles for consumer researchers whose work is still dominated by cognitive concepts.[52] It is interesting, in connection with this discussion of paradigms of choice, that Skinner describes behaviourism not as the science of human behaviour, but as 'the philosophy of that science'.[53]

Behaviour and its Control

The focus of behaviourism is behaviour itself rather than any mental antecedents or causes which may be attributed to it by cognitive psychologists. Interest in the prediction of responses from knowledge of stimuli alone (or the definition of stimuli exclusively from descriptions of responses) without recourse to the subjective introspection which was then the hallmark of American psychology, developed during the early years of this century. Watson made S–R relationships the fundamental unit of psychological analysis, abandoning so called mental phenomena such as attention, will and thought. In the consequent absence of introspective, subjective evidence and cognitively founded 'explanations' of action, behaviour was directly observed and described by a vocabulary shorn of references to inferred mental states. Miller points out that what the prevailing mentalistic psychologists called sensation and perception, Watson classed as no more than discriminatory responses; similarly, learning and memory were described in terms of the conditioning and maintenance of S–R links, thinking became talking and problem solving, motivation and valuing became choice behaviour, while emotion was understood in terms of the functioning of the autonomous nervous system, the glands and the muscles, 'Everything intangible was simply reduced to its most tangible manifestation.'[54] Indeed, thought itself became no more than sub-vocal verbalisation.

Two distinct emphases are apparent in the history of behaviourism. Concentration upon *S–R* associations lies at the heart of *classical* or *respondent* conditioning. 'Respondents' are involuntary response behaviours controlled by preceding stimuli. The well known experiments of Pavlov were concerned with the learning of conditioned responses, those which come to follow a stimulus which originally had no capacity to elicit them but which, after being continually linked with an unconditioned or 'natural' stimulus, are subsequently able to bring forth the conditioned response in the absence of other stimuli.[55] Typically a dog would be fed meat powder (unconditioned stimulus) shortly after a bell (the conditioned stimulus) had been rung; the response was salivation. Repetition of this procedure in which the conditioned and unconditioned stimuli were paired resulted in a situation in which the presentation of the auditory stimulus alone would produce salivation. The phenomena of classical conditioning apply also in the human sphere: the first time an individual listens to a new comedian his laughter is a response to the performer's material, but on subsequent occasions similar behaviour, smiling or laughter, is likely to accompany the mere sight of the comedian.[56]

Behaviourist analysis is not, however, confined to the study of classical conditioning. Skinner's approach, *operant* or *instrumental* conditioning, is based upon the observation that 'Behaviour is shaped and maintained by its consequences'.[57] Operants are behaviours which are conditioned by their consequences; since these consequences increase the likelihood of the operant's recurrence, strengthening the behaviour, they are known as reinforcers. Operant behaviours, as opposed to the reflexes elicited by stimuli in classical conditioning, are frequently described as voluntary: they are emitted by the individual who acts upon his environment and who receives the resulting, instrumental consequences.[58]

Whereas classical conditioning is concerned overwhelmingly with the antecedent environmental stimuli which cause behaviour, operant conditioning considers post behavioural effects of behaviour. The idea of reinforcement is central to behaviourist philosophy and its ramifications require further exposition if the role of this paradigm in marketing and consumer research is to be clarified.

A consequence which strengthens the behaviour which produced it is known as a *positive* reinforcer; *negative* reinforcement refers to the strengthening of behaviour which reduces or terminates the reinforcer. This distinction is sometimes critically confusing and an example may assist. A meal is positively reinforcing to a person who is hungry; if he then cooks and eats that meal, the probability of his repeating these behaviours in subsequently occurring similar circumstances increases. A gardener's removal of a painful thorn from his thumb is negatively reinforcing and his removal of thorns which cause him pain on other occasions becomes more predictable.[59] Positively reinforcing behaviour involves consequences such that the individual is likely to act in ways which elicit further, similar consequences; negatively reinforcing behaviour involves consequences which the individual will probably continue to avoid by operating upon his environment in ways which do not produce them.

The accumulation of behavioural consequences experienced by the individual thus constitute his reinforcement history which renders his subsequent behaviour in similar circumstances predictable. Within the behaviourist paradigm, the guiding principle is to the effect that the nature of past reinforcement determines the probability that a given operant behaviour will be repeated. The possibility of modifying the probabilities of occurrence of specific behaviour through the creation of an environment which 'rewards' operants with appropriate consequences thus arises. It is upon this possibility that the behavioural technology promoted by Skinner rests and from which any use of behaviourism in marketing stems.

Reinforcement and Behavioural Technology

This introduces another important term in behaviourist analysis: 'contingencies of reinforcement'. Skinner writes that, 'Behaviour which operates upon the environment to produce consequences ("operant" behaviour) can be studied by arranging environments in which specific consequences are contingent upon it.'[60] The significance of this in paradigmatic terms is evident from Skinner's assertion that 'The contingencies under investigation have become steadily more complex, and one by one they are taking over the explanatory functions previously assigned to personalities, states of mind, feelings, traits of character, purposes, and intentions.'[61] Indeed, the import of the behaviourist approach in the present context derives from its utterly distinct perspective of the causation and explanation of human behaviour and behaviour modification. Rather than attempt to modify or maintain behaviour by acting upon its alleged cognitive precursors and determinants, behaviourists advocate the manipulation of the environments within which response and reward occur – the conditions or contingencies of reinforcements. The result is an explanation of behaviour which attributes action, 'to the subtle and complex relations among . . . the situation in which behaviour occurs, the behaviour itself, and its consequences'.[62] It is within these three factors and their relations that contingencies of reinforcement inhere.

An important component of reinforcement contingencies which acts directly upon the repetition of operant behaviour is the relative frequency with which reinforcers are produced in response to such behaviour. There exist various 'schedules of reinforcement'. In continuous or fixed ratio reinforcement schedules every requisite operant behaviour is subsequently and appropriately rewarded, for example the warmth made available to the individual each time he stands before a fire. There is a one to one relation between the response and the reinforcer. Games of chance are based on an alternative schedule of reinforcement in which operant behaviour is rewarded only intermittently. The prediction of reinforcing occurrences is often rendered difficult or impossible in these circumstances, especially if the allocation of rewards is irregular or apparently random as in the case of fruit machines. The situation in which reinforcement *never* accompanies the performance of a particular operant leads (usually quickly) to the withdrawal of that behaviour by the individual, a phenomenon known as 'extinction'.

Behavioural science is presented by Skinner not simply as a means of describing and explaining the world as though these were self-sufficient acts but as the basis of a social technology, a means of shaping or controlling behaviour. It is in this respect that behaviourism is likely to be ultimately judged with respect to marketing management and consumer research and it is necessary now to indicate some of the procedures involved in behavioural technology.

While classical conditioning may proceed as a result of the production of stimuli which elicit particular responses, operant conditioning clearly cannot involve the reinforcement of behaviour until that behaviour appears. The problem, therefore, is to obtain the behaviour which is to be reinforced and this may be achieved by the shaping of behaviour through successive approximations. In animal experiments, the reinforcement of the extremely forceful pressing of a lever *could* be achieved by waiting for an extremely forceful push to occur and rewarding it appropriately; a quicker means is the extra reinforcement of the animal's more forceful actions with the result that the average amount of force employed in the depression of the lever is increased. Similar methods have been successfully employed in the treatment of patients in mental hospitals as well as in the shaping of human behaviour more generally.[63] Shaping demands the careful arrangement of reinforcement contingencies and schedules so that behaviour which increasingly approximates the required terminal behaviour is increasingly rewarded while behaviour which deviates from this pattern is not reinforced. This requires the identification and isolation of those differential aspects of the performance of a behavioural response which are to be reinforced and, if possible, their detailed specification. The result of shaping may be minor behavioural modification or novel and original behaviour.

Another means by which individuals acquire new patterns of behaviour is *modeling* in which he or she imitates the observed actions of others. Vicarious experience and learning may arise from the direct observation or description of the behaviour of others or from the mass media. The observation of the reinforcement of others' behaviour acts as a 'learning trial' for the observer.[64] This phenomenon is clearly associated with the generalisation of reinforced behaviour: once a behaviour has been reinforced in one set of circumstances, it is likely to appear in similar situations or even in situations which have only some features in common with those in which reinforcement occurred. If, however, behaviour is reinforced only when a particular environmental or situational feature, the individual learns to *discriminate*; the behaviour appears only when that factor is present in the situation and is said to be controlled by it. The arrangement of environments to modify behaviour, that is, the placing of stimuli and rewards in such a way as to elicit and reinforce behaviour of a given variety, is nowadays widely practised. Environmental or 'ecological' design involves the use of the phenomena of discrimination and generalisation in order to produce required patterns of behaviour.

Behaviourism in Consumer Research

Consumer research has made less use of behaviourist approaches than of cognitive information processing. The work of Howard has drawn extensively upon learning theory[65] and there are other quasi-behaviourist applications to the study of consumer choice,[66] but little systematic use and certainly no transfer of the psychological paradigm of behaviourism to marketing. However, insofar as marketing behaviour represents a microcosm of human social and economic behaviour in general it is possible to describe much buyer and managerial behaviour in terms of this paradigm and to cast prescriptions for consumer research accordingly. Nord and Peter, and Rothschild and Gaidis, to whom reference has been made, have attempted to show the relevance of behaviourism to these areas by indicating how accounts of current marketing practice may be recast in behaviourist terminology, by suggesting extensions of the use of behaviourist analysis in marketing management and research, and by identifying future academic and commercial research imperatives.[67]

Many of the actual and potential applications of the behaviourist framework of analysis and research to marketing may well have suggested themselves already to the reader. The following account illustrates these applications but is by no means exhaustive. Classical conditioning, which involves the pairing of environmental stimuli may be used in such a way as to associate stimuli like sporting events, to which the audience has learned a 'positive' or 'favourable' response with the attributes of a particular product or brand or with store characteristics. The incorporation of opinion leaders and other positive reference groups in advertising, sports event sponsorship, point of sale advertising and the use of in-store music and in television and radio commercials further exemplify the application of respondent conditioning techniques in which prior stimuli are expected to produce certain responses. There remains a deal of research to be conducted in this area, particularly experimentation with the deliberate pairing of stimuli to ascertain the actual effects of human respondent conditioning in the marketing context and, where valid and appropriate, to facilitate the more effective arrangement of stimuli.

Operant or instrumental conditioning, in which environments are so arranged that the consequences of particular behaviours reinforce those behaviours, probably offers a greater challenge to marketing managers and researchers. The use of rewards is already pervasive in marketing which, after all, depends vitally upon the provision of economic material reinforcers. Apart from the clear necessity to arrange product attributes so as to produce appropriate reinforcement of purchase and consumption patterns, marketers might do far more to operationalise facets of the Skinnerian paradigm by the more skilful arrangement of contingencies of reinforcement, that is, the circumstances and conditions in which behaviour occurs which determine its consequences and thus whether it will be repeated. Most economic reinforcers employed in marketing – notably in the form of product attributes – are arranged in schedules of continuous reinforcement. Every purchase or use of the item is intended to produce the same consequences and elaborate systems of quality control, efficient distribution and brand indentification are employed in order to ensure that positive reinforcement of consumer behaviour occurs on every occasion. Continuous reinforcement is invaluable in increasing the rate at which the learning of a new task occurs but subsequent consolidation of what is learned is usually better accomplished through the use of intermittent reinforcers. As far as product attributes are concerned, it would be an extremely dangerous strategy to make positive reinforcement contingent upon several brand trials; indeed the result would be that many purchases and consumptions would be negatively reinforced, customers turning to alternative brands which had previously been positively reinforcing. Rather than encouraging non-continuous reinforcement, behaviourist analysis in marketing encourages the use of quality control and consistent branding strategies. Individuals who are habitually reinforced on continuous schedules become extremely frustrated and depressed when the 'expected' reinforcement is not forthcoming.[68] The implication for marketing is that product quality and continuity are essential components of effective strategy.

Behaviourism in Marketing: Research Needs

It is evident, however, that the intentional use of behavioural technology in marketing demands a more substantial research base than is currently available. Little is known about the reinforcing effects of reinforcers of varying type and magnitude. Scott puts forward the intriguing hypothesis that there exists a continuum of effects: 'Experimental studies must include multiple levels of incentives over a broader range of magnitudes. The effects of incentives may or may not be linear, and are most likely related in some way to the price of the particular product.'[69] Related considerations to which consumer research should be addressed include the effectiveness of primary and secondary reinforcers, and of temporally immediate reinforcers compared with those which are delayed. Primary reinforcers, such as product attributes, have intrinsic utility while secondary reinforcers, such as coupons, have no intrinsic worth but must be exchanged in order to realise reinforcing benefits.

Rothschild and Gaidis suggest a sequence of various types of reinforcement which may provide an initial hypothesis for the testing of behaviourist approaches to consumer research and marketing management.[70] Their suggestion is that contingencies of reinforcement should be arranged so that the individual consumer is presented with the following sequence, say by a combination of product sampling, coupon offers and other 'deals' as well as primary product attributes, in order to assess the probabilities of behavioural change: immediate primary → immediate secondary or delayed primary → delayed secondary → no (extraneous) reinforcement. More fundamental questions also present themselves for empirical test: what reinforcement contingencies are linked with initial product trial? What is their reinforcing effect upon subsequent purchase? How should contingencies of reinforcement be arranged in order to increase the effectiveness of shaping and vicarious learning?

Many techniques are used in shaping whose use could be more effectively extended to the end of successive approximation. Loss leading, in-store competitions and related special offers are designed to create store loyalty. Free trials, credit terms, on approval trials, coupon offers and sampling permit the trial of products without which there can be no reinforcement. Shaping techniques carry the danger that secondary rather than primary reinforcers will be paramount and that the operant purchasing and consumption behaviours will be extinguished when the offers are withdrawn. The provision of opportunities for vicarious learning, for example, through in-store or domestic product demonstrations, assists in the education of consumers especially where innovative products are concerned, where familiar products are promoted in the context of novel uses, and where new patterns of shopping are encouraged. Connected with this may be the encouragement of the phenomena of discrimination (for example, through store logos, brand names, corporate images, with which previous positive reinforcement may become linked) and generalisation (for example, through advertisements drawing attention to past product/brand use). All of these techniques are and may be further employed in order to facilitate certain responses by consumers, encouraging the seeking of buyer-dominated information, for instance, where this may usefully complement that available through marketer-dominated channels. In certain circumstances, such as a shortage of raw materials, behaviourist techniques might be employed to decrease the demand for some products or brands. Marketers, especially retailers and planners, already practice environmental design in the arrangement of displays, the use of discriminative stimuli such as piped music, store location and shopping centre development. The deliberate employment of behaviourist techniques, when marketers find them reinforcing, would render such methods and approaches more effective, according to the advocates of the extension of their paradigm to marketing.

The most important implication of behaviourism to the present context, however, is the treatment of the concepts of attitude, attitude change and persuasion. The formation and changing of attitudes, which loom so large in cognitive information processes, are accorded little if any explicative power in behaviourism; mentalistic views of the effects of attitudes on overt behaviour are certainly absent from behaviourists' accounts of the antecedents and causes of behaviour.[71] Behaviourists are concerned rather with the conditioning of behaviours by the consequences: the verbal responses which provide the raw material of 'attitude data' in consumer research and much cognitive psychology are simply one sort of behaviour. Verbal and 'overt' behaviours are, according to this perspective, likely to be consistent with and predictable from each other only when their consequences coincide, when the individual makes no discrimination between the two classes of behaviour or their consequences.[72] If the word 'attitude' is employed at all in this framework, it refers either to verbal behaviour or to the consistency of behavioural responses towards an entity, recorded simply on the basis of observation of a series of behaviours.

This difference in perspective has immense implications for behavioural technology in general and for attempts to modify consumer behaviour in particular. While cognitive learning approaches are founded upon the assumption that the 'internalisation' of a persuasive message which modifies attitudes and other internal states or processes is a necessary prerequisite of behavioural change, behaviourist approaches point simply to the necessity of providing the reinforcement required if the behaviour is to be repeated or altered.

Many of these points of contact between behaviourism and marketing practice will be reconsidered in Chapters 4 and 5 which deal with the evidence for the usefulness of this and the cognitive information processing paradigms in marketing and in the final chapter which deals with the implications for marketing managers and consumer researchers of a paradigm shift. The remainder of this chapter discusses in preliminary terms the ways in which these paradigms may be compared and how their usefulness in both management and research depends upon their capacity to elucidate the empirical data which describe consumer choice.

A CHOICE OF PARADIGM?

The re-establishment of the cognitive paradigm in psychology and its displacement of behaviourism as the prevailing philosophy is now widely recognised by psychologists. Blumenthal speaks of the 'renaissance' of cognitive psychology,[73] while Neisser, in his text published in 1967, notes that 'A generation ago, a book like this one would have needed at least a chapter of self-defence against the behaviourist position. Today, happily, the climate of opinion has changed, and little or no defence is necessary.'[74] The justification for cognitive psychology is the asserted fact that 'Cognitive processes exist, so it can hardly be unscientific to study them.' The formal study of consumer behaviour in the context of marketing, based firmly upon the behavioural sciences, proliferated at a time when behaviourism was giving way to cognitive psychology as the dominant framework of conceptualisation and analysis. While behaviourism has far from disappeared – indeed some of the most incisive accounts of behaviourism as a scientific philosophy or paradigm have been published since 1970 – by the time consumer researchers began to 'borrow' heavily from psychology in the 1960s, it had ceased to dominate psychological explanation.

Although behaviourism has had some effect upon the development of marketing thought and, as has been pointed out above, is implicit in much marketing practice, it has not until recently been considered an alternative framework for consumer research generally.

The explanations of behaviour provided by cognitive psychology and behaviourism posit antithetical views of the acquisition of behaviour and of the appropriate approach to the modification of behaviour. Yet each appears to be consistent with a view of how marketing works and thus to suggest valid prescriptions for managerial action. One places the locus of behavioural control resolutely within the individual, 'its proponents try to identify precisely various cognitive states, mechanisms, and processes, and to characterise attitudes and behaviours in the light of their informational determinants.'[75] The other locates the determinants of behaviour equally resolutely in the

external environment, both as it supposedly shaped the evolution of
the species by eliciting the behaviour and development upon which
the survival of the species was contingent and (more importantly for a
technology of behaviour) as it currently controls behaviour by em-
bodying contingencies of behavioural reinforcement. Skinner emphasises the crucial difference between himself and both the cognitive
scientists and those behaviourists who adopted intervening explicative variables in terms of the locus of control of behaviour, 'For me the
observable operations in conditioning lay *outside* the organism, but
Tolman put them inside, as replacements for, if not simply redefi-
nitions of, mental processes, and that is where they still are in cognitive psychology today.'[76]

The common use of a given paradigm in science is evidently related
to shared beliefs about what exists to be studied and the nature of the
relations among its elements. But no paradigm comprehends all
known facts. Rather, it is the result of selection among those facts and
relations which promise to repay most abundantly further study.
Paradigms are thus based upon expediency as well as current under-
standings of the phenomenal universe. 'Radical' behaviourists such
as Skinner do not deny the existence of what cognitive psychologists
call mental processes but they firmly dispute their description in mental terms. Feelings are interpreted as inner, physiological processes
which are the by-products of behaviour but not reinforcers; attention
refers not to sensory stimulation but to the contingencies upon which
the process of discrimination is based; memory and recall refer to the
familiarity of past experiences in the light of current environmental
stimuli; problem solving is the means by which the individual de-
velops a response which produces a 'desired' reinforcement: the problem lasts only as long as the requisite response is not available. Although 'methodological' behaviourists range from those who deny
outright the existence of mental events to those who only deny their
usefulness in scientific analysis and ignore them because of the inability of researchers to agree about their nature and significance ,
radical behaviourists reposition some alleged intrapersonal factors
and reinterpret others.

As this chapter has also shown, not all behaviourists eschew assumed organo-centric factors even to the extent that radical behaviourists do, and there are numerous psychologists who attempt to
combine cognitive and behavioural approaches. Behaviourism has
been discussed here in radical terms, however, because this frame-

work serves to distinguish it from cognitive approaches and it is the radical behaviourist philosophy which has been most clearly articulated of late. This book is concerned, nevertheless, with cognitive and behaviourist paradigms at their broadest. How is consumer research to discriminate between them and which set of principles should guide marketing management?

SUMMARY AND CONCLUSION

Although it is not possible to establish or refute a scientific paradigm by direct, empirical investigation normal science proceeds within a framework which is accepted because it is generally believed to be consistent with and/or explain the available evidence. If the larger proportion of the evidence cannot be reconciled with the prevailing paradigm, then modification or replacement of that paradigm is in order. Paradigm shift may occur when (i) new results which are quite incapable of interpretation within the existing framework are incorporated in a new paradigm along with whatever previous data, theories and methodologies can be harmoniously accommodated or (ii) when novel, superior explanations reveal the inadequacies of prevailing frameworks of conception and analysis. Tracing the progress of competing paradigms is, nevertheless, an immense task and can be fully accomplished only retrospectively. The purpose of this book is more modest than this and is essentially exploratory rather than definitive.

While it draws extensively upon social psychology, it is ultimately concerned with marketing. Specifically, it is concerned with the treatment of attitudes and behaviour in consumer research. The relationship between these is perhaps the most important in consumer research carried out within the cognitive information processing framework. The empirical demonstration of attitudinal–behavioural consistency is crucial to the continued acceptance of the cognitive paradigm. Unless actual or hypothetical intrapersonal states prefigure and determine behaviour the edifice of contemporary marketing theory must begin to crumble. If additional concepts and empirical data have to be taken into consideration in an alternative explanation of behaviour, the obvious conclusion is that the cognitive paradigm has been modified or replaced. The following chapter examines critically the prevailing view of the nature of marketing (especially marketing communication) as a persuasive force which acts upon consumer behaviour through the antecedent modification of their attitudes, and contrasts this with the view that any influence on behaviour effected by marketing and advertising is relatively weak and occurs by reinforcing experience rather than by the alteration of mental states.

The appropriate paradigm within which to undertake consumer research and the marketing management which relies upon it will, among other things, provide an interpretation of attitudinal–behavioural dynamics which is consistent with psychological and marketing theory that is derived from the available empirical evidence. How can we discover which paradigm is the more adequate for the explanation of actual attitudinal-behavioural relationships? As Jacoby has said, 'No other single psychological construct has permeated consumer research as has the construct of attitude.'[77] The answer to this question is thus of immense paradigmatic significance in consumer research and marketing management.

Chapter 3

The Behaviour of Consumers' Attitudes

CONCEPTS OF ATTITUDE

To refer to the tendency or inclination to behave consistently in some particular way as an 'attitude' or as corresponding to an 'attitude' is to use the term metaphorically. 'Attitude' implied originally the literal leaning of a building or bodily posture and has only comparatively recently been used to describe behaviour, opinions or their underlying patterns of thought. Figurative uses of words are seldom as rigorously circumscribed as their literal applications and there is a range of definitions of attitude in psychology and marketing. There is some agreement that the term refers to 'a learned predisposition to respond in a consistently favourable or unfavourable manner with respect to a given object' but, as Fishbein and Ajzen demonstrate, even this is a highly ambiguous statement and permits a variety of methodologies and explanations of behaviour.[1]

Numerous competing theories of attitude have been advanced during the past thirty years, a fact which confirms the impression that this field of social psychology is at a critical stage of development. Cognitive consistency theories have appeared in several versions, for example the dissonance theory of Festinger and the affective–consistency approach of Rosenberg which challenged the balance theory of Heider and the congruity theory of Osgood and Tannenbaum.[2] Learning theories and, in particular the behaviouristic self-perception theory of Bem, have provided distinctive explanations of observed events.[3] Social judgement theories, attribution theory, and functional theory have also been devised to account for the same phenomena[4] and some of these have found echoes in the marketing literature.[5] The reference to Kuhn's description of a science in crisis is justified further by the proliferation of *ad hoc* empirical investigations of attitudes and behaviour. The critical state of attitude research is only too clear from the various arguments adduced in favour of definitions and general notions of the structure of attitudes – from the representation of attitudes as tricomponential amalgams of cognition, affect and conation, to their consideration in terms of just cognition and affect, to the restriction of the term to refer to affect alone.[6]

Fortunately, in order to approach the issue of how far the cognitive and behaviourist paradigms respectively account for the evidence about attitudinal–behavioural relationships, it is necessary only to derive broad conceptions of attitude which are consistent with each of these frameworks in turn. From these general conceptions, criteria by which the empirical evidence may be classified and interpreted may be derived.

Probability and Latent Process Conceptions

In their influential paper on the scientific status of attitudes, DeFleur and Westie distinguish two conceptions of attitude which are respectively expressed in definitions: these are probability conceptions and latent process conceptions.[7] A probability conception is concerned with the consistency of behavioural responses and derives from the observation that a set of responses to a particular object exhibits a degree of consistency and thus predictability. The term 'attitude' refers simply to the probability that a particular behavioural response will recur in reaction to a given object or stimulus and this probability is inferred directly from observations of previous behaviour in similar circumstances. As these authors point out, any definition based upon a probability conception, '*anchors the attitude concept* firmly to observable events . . . The attitude, then is an inferred property of the responses, namely their consistency. Stated in another way, attitude is equated with the probability of recurrence of behaviour forms of a given type or direction.'[8] Use of the word 'attitude' is consequently confined to the description of observable behaviour in terms of the extent to which it shows consistency over time.

The latent process conception goes beyond the observation of response consistency by positing an intrapersonal function or process which intervenes between the stimulus object and the responsive behaviour, causing or at least acting upon it, shaping and guiding it. In the words of DeFleur and Westie:

the observable organisation of behaviour is said to be 'due to' or can be 'explained by' the action of some mediating *latent* variable. The attitude, then, is not the manifest responses themselves, or their probability, but an intervening variable operating between stimulus and response and inferred from the overt behaviour. This inner process is seen as giving both direction and consistency to the person's response.[9]

This is the most widely encountered understanding of attitude in social psychology where 'The implicit assumption has usually been of a simple, causal relationship between a multidimensional conception of attitude towards a social object and specific behaviour towards the object, irrespective of situation.'[10] Like the paradigm to which it belongs, this is now the conventional wisdom, for 'Most psychologists', according to Reich and Adcock, 'take the view that a concept such as attitude is best viewed as an "intervening" or "mediating" variable. By this is meant that we have to posit a construct which we assume to exist but which is not directly observable.'[11]

Nevertheless, inferences about the nature of attitude must eventually be related to the observable responses which are assumed to be caused by attitude and to be consistent with it over a range of situations. A similar remark with respect to the nonobservability of attitudes is made in the context of consumer behaviour by Walters who nevertheless claims that 'we must make the attempt to understand attitudes because they guide everyday consumer actions. People seldom act in opposition to their attitudes, just as they seldom go against their motives.'[12] And, again in the realm of consumer research, Day endorses the conception of attitude as an unobservable mediating or intervening construct which is linked to two forms of observable factors, 'One link is with the *antecedent* conditions which lead to it; these might be the stimulus of an advertisement, a move to a new house, and so forth. The second link is with the *consequents* that follow from the attitude, including search and purchase behaviour.'[13] All of these statements are in alignment with the definition of attitude devised by Allport which has had the most profound effect upon both social psychology and marketing, 'An attitude is a mental and neural state of readiness, organised through experience, exerting a directive or dynamic influence upon the individual's response to all objects and situations with which it is related.'[14]

Each of these conceptions has direct and specific implications for attitudinal–behavioural consistency. The latent process conception

leads logically to the expectation of consistency between 'verbal' behaviour (the responses made to attitude measuring devices such as
questionnaires) and 'overt' behaviour, both of which are responses
which, if directed towards the same object, ought to be consistent
since the identical latent process mediates both. The stable, underlying mechanisms of behaviour postulated by latent process theorists
who depict attitude change as a slow, resistant procedure, cause all
classes of response to the objects they govern regardless of whether
those responses are verbal or active. The consistency which is the
hallmark of the latent process approach should be manifest in both
types of *behaviour*.

The verbal responses which are usually taken to be measures of underlying attitudes ought to correlate highly with and predict accurately the active responses which are also the result of the attitude.[15]
The underlying, unobservable mental mechanism or process which
comprises the individual's attitude (sometimes called his 'true' attitude) is, according to the latent process conception, equally causative of the various behaviours of that individual with respect to the re-
ferrent object. In the case of probability conceptions of attitude, however, consistency is simply a question of empirical observation, a matter of determining by relatively straightforward recording the probabilities of the occurrence of various classes of response in given circumstances. Observed inconsistency between what an individual
says and what he does about an object would pose no problem of
theory, concept, or method since the verbal and overt responses belong to different classes of behaviour, each occurring in accord with its
peculiar set of situational contingencies. Thus DeFleur and Westie
describe attitudes as, 'specific *probabilities* of specific forms of response
to specific social objects'.[16]

Implications for Attitudes and Behaviour

The terms 'latent process conception' and 'probability conception' do
not in themselves denote specific definitions of attitude but refer to conceptual categories from which definitions and operational categories
derive. These conceptual categories derive, in turn, from paradigms.
The latent process view has its origins in cognitive psychology, the
psychology of internal information processing which asserts that behaviour results and is predictable from knowledge of antecedent, intrapersonal states. The probability conception makes no such attri-

bution of prebehavioural, intervening processes. It belongs to the broad paradigm of behaviourism. It is placed there in a review of De-Fleur and Westie's paper by Alexander who states that their definition:

> anchors attitude to the specific, external stimulus situations in which the individual responds. Attitude has been regarded as an inner-state variable that exists dispositionally, but the authors are denying its independence of the specific stimulus situations in which responses are observed. Consequently, as Skinner (1953) observed long ago, an inner-state directly expressed and totally exhausted by the probability of a class of responses is conceptually superfluous; it is necessary only to deal directly with the response probabilities.[17]

Neither does the probability conception lead to inferences of a simple, causal relationship between attitudes and behaviour or between different classes of behavioural response regardless of contextual differences which arise from situational factors and contingencies of reinforcement. The closer the correspondence between the situations within which verbal and overt responses to a stimulus object occur, however, the greater is the probability of response similarity and consistency. While, in the latent process conception of attitude, attitudinal change is causative and a necessary antecedent of behavioural change, probability conception theorists assume that behavioural change occurs as a result of the patterns of reinforcement encountered in consequence of past behaviour or as a result of changes in reinforcement contingencies.

The idea of causality implies that one variable produces another or that a change in one variable can produce consistent change in another in the absence of extraneous changes in contextual factors.[18] There are four possible causal relationships between attitudes and behaviour: (i) attitudes cause behaviours, (ii) behaviours cause attitudes, (iii) attitudes and behaviours are reciprocally causative, or (iv) attitudes and behaviours are unrelated. Each of these propositions is supported by at least one eminent psychologist who adduces empirical evidence and theoretical explanation in favour of his stance.[19] Any pattern of association is compatible with definitions derived from the probability conception of attitude since causality is ascribed to environmental factors rather than internal, mediating states. Definitions derived from the latent process conception are, however, compatible with the proposition that there is a causal relationship between attitudes and behaviour which is uni-directional from attitudes to behaviour and is not altered by environmental factors.

This would, however, be a very stringent criterion by which to judge the data on attitudinal–behavioural relationships. The problem of establishing the direction of any causation beyond doubt is immense given the deficiencies of current methodologies.[20] Fortunately, it is possible to compare latent process and probability conceptions in terms of the evidence without formulating a definition that is either untestable or simplistic. While correlational evidence of attitudinal–behavioural consistency 'irrespective of situations' is not sufficient to demonstrate a causal relationship, it is certainly necessary to that demonstration. If the latent process conception is valid, therefore, variance in attitudinal measures will explain statistically all the variance in corresponding behavioural measures: at the very least, given the noise surrounding the data, very high correlations between attitudes (verbal statements or opinions) and corresponding behaviour should be found since the assumption is that both are mediated by the same underlying, 'true' attitude or latent process. But the more necessary it becomes to add explanatory variables in regressions of behaviour on attitude, the less satisfactory the explanation prompted by the latent process conception of attitudinal–behavioural relations must be adjudged. The increasing need to employ contextual variables to account for behaviour patterns would render the probability conception more and more appropriate as an explicative device.

ATTITUDINAL–BEHAVIOURAL CONSISTENCY

The expectation that attitudes constitute, 'precursors of behaviour, . . . determinants of how a person will actually behave in his daily affairs'[21] remains strong, as the prevalence of latent process conceptions attests. Even the vivid demonstration by LaPiere that verbal statements of intention to act in a given way (in this case with regard to the accommodation of a Chinese couple in an American hotel or restaurant) can fail dramatically to vary with actual behaviour[22] has not expunged this expectation. LaPiere obtained statements that most restaurateurs and hoteliers were unwilling to accommodate such a couple, *after* they had experienced overwhelming success in being so received): his findings still haunt sociologists and social psychologists but have done nothing to arrest the growth of empirical research directed towards the practical demonstration of attitudinal–behavioural consistency.

A critical review by Wicker of a portion of the literature derived from this research[23] sums up the disappointment of most investigators during the mid to late 1960s. Wicker examined forty six empirical studies of attitudes and behaviour, selected so that individuals were the unit of observation, at least one attitudinal measure and one temporally-separate measure of behaviour towards a common object was taken of each subject, and overt behaviour was not measured simply by subjects' post behavioural self-report. Studies of attitudinal and behavioural change were excluded. The chosen investigations covered a diversity of verbal measures of attitude: Thurstone's method of equal-appearing intervals, the summated ratings technique, devised by Likert, Osgood, Suci and Tannenbaum's semantic differential, and interviews.[24] A range of measures of behavioural response (for example willingness to be photographed with a member of a racial minority, attendance at meetings, cheating in examinations) is also apparent from the studies reviewed. In addition, there was a wide selection of sampling frames (including maternity patients, union members, students and oilfield workers). But Wicker's conclusions could not be more damaging for psychologists who adopt the latent process conception.

'Taken as a whole', he writes:

> these studies suggest that it is considerably more likely that attitudes will be unrelated or only slightly related to actions. Product-moment correlation coefficients relating the two kinds of responses are rarely above 0.30, and are often nearer zero. Only rarely can as much as 10 per cent of the variance in overt behaviour measures be accounted for by attitudinal data. In studies in which data are dichotomised, substantial proportions of subjects show attitude–behaviour discrepancies. This is true even when subjects scoring at the extremes of attitudinal measures are compared on behavioural indices.[25]

Wicker's review also failed to establish the existence of a predictable pattern of causation between the attitudinal and behavioural

variables. Six studies indicated that when measures of overt behaviour or behavioural commitment preceded the measurement of attitudes, attitudinal–behavioural consistency was greater than when
this procedure was reversed; but four others demonstrated inconsistencies.

Such conclusions as these cast considerable gloom on both social
psychological and marketing research since both had been firmly predicated upon the expectation that a demonstrable relationship
existed. While some psychologists and market researchers argued
that the conclusion that attitudes never predicted behaviour was too
dire, others appeared prepared to dispense altogether with the concept of attitude.[26] It is then superficially surprising to find reviews of
the attitude–behaviour literature a few years later reporting a rather
different state of affairs. A much greater spirit of optimism is apparent
in these accounts.[27] Schuman and Johnson conclude, for example,
that, 'Our review has shown that most *A–B* [attitude–behaviour]
studies yield positive results. The correlations that do occur are large
enough to indicate that important causal forces are involved.'[28] And
Seibold notes the moderate to strong correlational consistency indicated by numerous empirical studies concluded since the publication
of Wicker's analysis.[29]

'Other Variables', Correspondence and Consistency

The reasons for this transformation are not difficult to find. DeFleur
and Westie argued convincingly that definitions of attitude should be
more closely linked with the methods employed in attitude measurement:

> Exact specification of the class of response (verbal, overt, emo
> tional–autonomic) would aid considerably in the clarification of
> thinking concerning the degree to which predictions can be made
> from one class of response to another. The fallacy of expected cor
> respondence resulted historically from the conception of attitudes
> as *general* response tendencies which implied that consistency
> should appear from one class of behaviour to another, that verbal
> attitudes 'should' predict overt behaviour. It has taken a quarter
> century of research . . . to refute this conception. Attitudes appear
> to be most usefully conceptualised as *specific*, in the sense that they
> may be viewed as probabilities of specific forms of response to
> specific social objects, or specific classes of social objects.[30]

This would, of course, detract from the use of intervening constructs to predict behaviour. Wicker[35] points out, moreover, that most investigators of attitudinal–behavioural reltionships argue that factors other than attitudes impinge upon the measured behaviour and that these 'other factors' must, therefore, be considered when behaviour is predicted. *Personal factors*, which include other attitudes, compelling motives, and verbal, intellectual and social abilities, and *situational factors* such as the actual or assumed presence of other people, normative prescriptions of proper behaviour, alternative available behaviours, lack of specificity of the attitude objects, unforeseen extraneous events and the actual or expected consequences of various acts, have all been suggested as causes of the inconsistency encountered between measures of attitudes and behaviour. Methodological problems have also been noted as contributing to the disappointing results of the search for attitudinal–behavioural consistency, though these often reflect lack of attention to variation in situational variables. Thus the selected attitude measure, behavioural criterion, and the circumstances in which both are measured may lead to the collection of incomparable data.[32]

The optimism of those psychologists who have reported relatively high levels of attitudinal–behavioural consistency derives, according to Seibold from research in which the relationships between circumstantial factors and measured levels of attitudinal–behavioural consistency have been carefully identified and specified.[33] Table 3.1 summarises the 'other variables' employed in this research. The first two sections of this table are concerned with the measurement of attitudes and behaviour in ways which render the correspondence and congruity of the measured variables probable on more than simplistic, intuitive grounds. Schuman and Johnson set particularly high standards for the contextual framework within which attitudinal–behavioural consistency may be genuinely inferred, independently of researcher or experimenter effects:

> Methodologically, a fully adequate investigation of an A–B [attitudinal–behavioural] relationship should involve measuring actual behaviour objectively and unobtrusively, without signalling in any way its connection to the prior or subsequent attitude assessment phase . . . Ideally, attitude and behaviour need to be measured in ways that dissociate the two completely in the subject's mind, or else the need to present a temporarily consistent picture may result in spuriously high A–B relationships.[34]

Table 3.1 *Factors increasing measured attitudinal–behavioural consistency*

ATTITUDE MEASURES

1. The attitude measure should be con-   Heberlein and Black,
structed with the same level of speci-   Weigel, Vernon & Tognacci
ficity as the behavioural criterion; this   Wicker & Pomezal
replaces the practice of employing gen-   Fishbein & Ajzen Schwarz
eral measures of attitude towards the
object to predict particular behaviours.

2. Attitude towards the act should be   Fishbein & Ajzen
measured rather than attitude   Peterson & Dutton
towards the object; act or situation-   Rokeach & Kliejunas
specific measures with the latter may,
however, increase predictive value.

3. Multiple-item attitude scales should   Tittle & Hill
be used.   (but cf. Schuman & Johnson)

4. Measurement error or inter-measure-   Alwin
ment change should be considered.   McPhee & Seibold

BEHAVIOURAL CONCEPTUALISATION

1. Consistency correlations are higher   Fishbein & Ajzen
when general attitude measures are   Weigel & Newman
used to predict multi-act behavioural
criteria *and* when specific measures of
attitude are employed in the
prediction of single act behavioural
criteria. The latter produce
higher correlations than the
former and measures of attitude
towards the act increase correlation coefficients.

2. Close correspondence between   Ajzen & Fishbein
attitudes and behaviours
increases correlated consistency.

3. Attitude measures provide better   Schuman & Johnson
predictions of symbolic behav-
iours such as making a commitment than of actual experience
with the attitude object.

4. Consistency is higher when the   Crespi
behaviour measured is highly   Tittle & Hill
institutionalised, routine or   Schuman & Johnson
familiar, when individuals can   Ehrlich
foresee their behaviour and are
willing to reveal their behavioural
intentions.

Table 3.1   *continued*

5. Measured consistency is higher, the shorter the time interval between the measurement of the variables.	Fishbein Davidson & Jaccard Schwarz

CONTEXTUAL AND MODERATING VARIABLES
Schuman and Johnson (1976, pp. 185–99) show that

1. The degree of consistency varies according to the attitude object and situation.	Bern & Allen Davey
2. Normative beliefs may influence behaviour both separately from and conjointly with attitudes.	Andrews & Kandel
3. Immediate social pressures impinge on attitude-behaviour correspondence in a manner consistent or inconsistent with previously measured attitudes.	Fields & Schuman Norman
4. Privately expressed attitudes may not be consistent with public behaviour.	Green
5. A–B consistency varies directly with attitudinal certainty confidence salience intensity internal consistency and stability	Sample and Warland Fazio & Zanna Brown Petersen & Dutton Norman Schwarz
6. Inconsistency between one's own attitudes and those perceived as belonging to reference groups decreases personal A–B consistency.	Frideres, Warner & Albrecht
7. Attitudes whose formation results from direct, personal experience show greater consistency with relevant behaviours than those formed through indirect experience.	Regan & Fazio, Songer-Nocks

CONCEPTUALISATION OF CONSISTENCY

Literal consistency is no longer expected. Previous failures to establish consistency were often based upon the expectation of an isomorphic relationship between verbal and overt behaviours. Correlational consist-	Schuman & Johnson

Contin. overleaf

Table 3.1 *continued*

---

tency, which indicates the extent to
which individuals are ordered on both
measures, is now generally sought and
acknowledges that consistency may be
rediated by factors extrinsic to attitude–
behaviour relationships'.

Source: Derived from Seibold, 'Attitude–Verbal Report–Behaviour Relationships as
Causal Processes', pp. 211–13.

The full references to cited works are as follows:

T. A. Heberlin and J. S. Black, 'Attitudinal Specificity and the Prediction of Behaviour
in a Field Setting', *Journal of Personality and Social Psychology*, vol. 33 (1976) pp. 474–9;
R. H. Weigel, T. A. Vernon and L. N. Tognacci, 'The Specificity of the Attitude as a
Determinant of Attitude–Behaviour Congruence', *Journal of Personality and Social
Psychology*, vol. 30 (1974) pp. 724–8; A. W. Wicker and R. J. Pomazal, 'The Relationship Between Attitudes and Behaviour as a Function of Specificity of Attitude Object
and Presence of Significant Person During Assessment Condition', *Representative
Research in Social Psychology*, vol. 2 (1971) pp. 26–31; M. Fishbein and I. Ajzen, 'Attitudes
towards Objects as Predictors of Single and Multiple Behavioural Criteria', *Psychological Review*, vol. 81 (1974) pp. 59–74; S. Schwartz, 'Temporal Instability as a Moderator
of the Attitude–Behaviour Relationship', *Journal of Personality and Social Psychology*, vol.
36, (1978) pp. 715–24; Fishbein and Ajzen, *Belief, Attitude, Intention and Behaviour*; K.
Petersen and J. E. Dutton, 'Centrality, Extremity and Intensity', *Social Forces*, vol. 54,
(1975) pp. 393–414; M. Rokeach and P. Kliejunas, 'Behaviour as a Function of
Attitude–towards–Object and Attitude–toward–Situation', *Journal of Personality and
Social Psychology*, vol. 22 (1972) pp. 194–201; Tittle and Hill, 'Attitude Measurement
and Prediction of Behaviour'; Schuman and Johnson, 'Attitudes and Behaviour'; D. F.
Alwin, 'Making Inferences from Attitude–Behaviour Correlations', *Sociometry*, vol. 36
(1973) pp. 253–78; D. F. Alwin, 'Attitude Scales as Congeneric Tests', *Sociometry*, vol.
39, (1976) pp. 377–83; R. D. McPhee and D. R. Seibold, 'Rationale, Procedures, and
Applications for Decomposition of Explained Variance in Multiple Regression
Analyses', *Communications Research*, vol. 6 (1979) pp. 345–84; R. H. Weigel and L. S.
Newman, 'Increasing Attitude–Behaviour Correspondence by Broadening the Scope
of the Behavioural Measure', *Journal of Personality and Social Psychology*, vol. 33 (1976) pp.
793–802; I. Crespi, 'What Kinds of Attitude Measure are Predictive of
Behaviour?', *Public Opinion Quarterly*, vol. 35 (1971) pp. 327–34; H. T. Ehrlich,
'Attitudes, Behaviour and the Intervening Variables', *American Sociologist*, vol. 4 (1969)
pp. 35–41; A. R. Davidson and J. J. Jaccard, 'Variables that Moderate the Attitude–
Behaviour Relation', *Journal of Personality and Social Psychology*, vol. 37 (1979) pp. 146–70;
A. Davey, 'Attitudes and the Prediction of Social Conduct', *British Journal of Social and
Clinical Psychology*, vol. 15 (1976) pp. 11–22; K. H. Andrews and D. B. Kandel,
'Attitude and Behaviour', *American Sociological Review*, vol. 44 (1979) pp. 298–310; J.
Fields and H. Schuman, 'Public Beliefs about the Beliefs of the Public', *Public Opinion
Quarterly*, vol. 40 (1977) pp. 427–48; R. Norman, 'Affective–Cognitive Consistency,
Conformity and Behaviour', *Journal of Personality and Social Psychology*, vol. 32 (1975) pp.
83–91; J. A. Green, 'Attitudinal and Situational Determinants of Intended Behaviour
towards Blacks', *Journal of Personality and Social Psychology*, vol. 22 (1972) pp. 13–17; J.
Sample and R. Warland, 'Attitude and the Prediction of Behaviour', *Social Forces*, vol.
51 (1973) pp. 292–304; R. H. Fazio and M. P. Zanna, 'Attitudinal Qualities Relating

to the Strength of the Attitude–Behaviour Relationship', *Journal of Experimental Social Psychology*, vol. 14 (1978) pp. 398–408; D. Brown, 'Adolescent Attitudes and Lawful Behaviour', *Public Opinion Quarterly*, vol. 38 (1974) pp. 98–106; J. Frideres, L. Warner and L. Albrecht, 'The Impact of Constraints on the Relationship between Attitudes and Behaviour', *Social Forces*, vol. 50 (1971) pp. 102–12; D. T. Regan and R. Fazio, 'On the Consistency between Attitudes and Behaviour', *Journal of Experimental Social Psychology*, vol. 13 (1977) pp. 28–45; E. Songer-Nocks, 'Situational Factors Affecting the Weighting of Predictor Components in the Fishbein Model', *Journal of Experimental Social Psychology*, vol. 12 (1976) pp. 56–69.

Their review, not surprisingly, contains reference to few studies which attain this ideal but it remains a useful benchmark by which to assess deviations in evaluating the results of empirical studies.

With or without this ideal level of dissociation, however, studies of attitudinal–behavioural relationships report greater consistency the greater the correspondence between the measures of attitude employed and the measures of behaviour. Ajzen and Fishbein argue that attitudinal and behavioural phenomena each comprise four elements: the *action*, the *target* of that action, the *context* within which the action occurs and the *time* at which it takes place.[35] (Fishbein has long argued that attitudes towards performing a specific behaviour with respect to an object should be measured rather than the much more general attitude towards the object.)

Correspondence between the attitudinal predictor and the behavioural criterion depends upon the degree to which the attitude measure matches the behavioural measure on these four elements. Consistent strength in the relationship between an individual's attitude and his behaviour is found when both are directed towards an identical target and both refer to the same action. (Ajzen and Fishbein's review concentrates upon studies fulfilling these two criteria of correspondence because so few investigators provide data about the others.) Their results for the 142 studies of attitudes and behaviour they review are summarised in Table 3.2. It may be argued that the criterion upon which the level of attitudinal–behavioural consistency is judged to be high or low is not especially rigorous. If $r = 0.40$, only 16 per cent of behavioural variance has been explained in terms of attitude. There are, furthermore, dangers in aggregating the correlation coefficients obtained in diverse investigations. But it is clear from this table that the authors' general point has been made: to put it in its least persuasive form, when correspondence is low, so is the correlational consistency between attitudes and behaviour.

Furthermore, the twenty six studies in the high correspondence condition which employed 'appropriate measures' all showed high levels of attitudinal–behavioural relationship.

Table 3.2   *Correspondence and attitudinal–behavioural consistency*

Attitudinal-behavioural relationship	Level of correspondence		
	Low	Partial	High
Not significant	26	20	0
Low or inconsistent (r < 0.40)	1	47	9
High (r ⩾ 0.40)	0	4	35

Source: I. Ajzen and M. Fishbein, 'Attitude-Behaviour Relations: A Theoretical Analysis and Review of Empirical Research', *Psychological Bulletin*, vol. 84 (1977) p. 913.

Behavioural Intentions and Behaviour

The third section of Table 3.1 refers to the 'other variables' which have been increasingly studied in the wake of disappointment over the inability of empirical research to demonstrate sufficiently convincing levels of attitudinal–behavioural consistency to substantiate the latent process idea. Any serious attempt at arguing in favour of attitudes as latent processes on the basis of the evidence of hundreds of field studies is severely qualified by the inclusion of a broad range of constraints which reflect the need for attitude and behaviour measures to correspond very specifically, to treat behaviour in a given situation, and to take into account the direct effects of situational variables upon behaviour. Seibold who is an able exponent of the latent process conception concedes that, 'Behaviours are a consequence of personal, social and environmental influences, and attitudes are but one of the factors affecting action'.[36] He proposes that theory must treat, 'situated actions in terms of specific configurations of those influences'.[37]

In the review which cast grave doubts upon the expectation of attitudinal–behavioural consistency, Wicker noted that the possibility that non–attitudinal factors entered significantly into the determination of overt behaviour was commonly assumed, especially by researchers who had attempted and failed to establish that consistency empirically.[38] The actual effects of these 'other variables' were, at that time, largely unsubstantiated by research findings, however, though Wicker concluded that, 'once these variables are operationalised, their contribution and the contribution of attitude to the variance of overt behaviour can be determined'.[39] The extent to which this has been the case in the interim can be judged by consideration of an approach to the attitude–behaviour problem which has been variously described as 'fashionable', 'a fad' and 'the most influential model' in applied psychology: Fishbein's behavioural intentions model which Fishbein and Ajzen[40] now present in the context of a 'theory of reasoned action'.

While it was originally derived from the theory of propositional control put forward by Dulany and has much in common with the version of expectancy–value theory advanced by Rosenberg,[41] the Fishbein model, from its inception to its most recent theoretical and methodological elaborations, has played a distinct role in the study of attitudes and behaviour in both social psychology and marketing.[42] Fishbein defines attitude solely in terms of affect (overall evaluation) while defining cognitions in terms of the beliefs of which attitudes are a function, and conation as the behavioural intentions which mediate overt behaviour. He avoids the classic problem of attitudinal–behavioural consistency in social psychology which is framed in terms of the relationship between attitudes towards an object and subsequent behaviour towards that object. He argues that individuals hold a multiplicity of attitudes towards an object and there is no reason why any one of them should predict all of the possible behaviour patterns of that individual with respect to the object. Rather he concentrates upon the individual's attitude towards performing a given behaviour or act with respect to the object in closely defined circumstances. Thus, rather than enquire simply of attitudes towards, say, frozen peas, the consumer researcher might pose questions or attitude statements which enquire specifically of the use of frozen peas as part of a family meal or a dinner party or in salads, or of their purchase in defined quantities, at given prices, from particular retail outlets. Attitude towards the act is expressed in terms of an expectancy–value model thus:

$$A act = \sum_{i=1}^{n} B_i a_i$$

where $A act$ = the attitude towards the act
B = the individual's belief that the behaviour in question will result in outcome i

a = his evaluation of (or attitude towards) outcome i
and n = the number of beliefs.[43]

The Behavioural Intentions Model

In the extended model, known also as the Fishbein behavioural intentions model, behavioural intentions are posited as a function of attitudes towards performing an act in a specific situation (as defined above) plus the subject's normative beliefs about the social expediency of performing this act as they are aroused by his motivation to comply with the social norms as he perceives them. Thus, neither behavioural intentions nor the behaviour they are assumed to approximate is depicted simply and exclusively as a function of attitude. This alone places the Fishbein model beyond the scope of simple attitudinal–behavioural relationships.

The effects of social environment on behaviour are accounted for in the behavioural intentions model by a term which subsumes the individual's expectations that a specific reference group's members expect him to behave in the particular manner under investigation. Since different reference groups make various demands on the individual, some of which he ignores in order to reduce role conflict, his motivation to comply with the expectations of specified reference groups is used to weight the normative beliefs component. The intentions theory thus takes the following form when a single or generalised significant other is assumed:

$$B \simeq BI = [Aact]w_0 + [NB\,(M_c)]w_1$$

where B = overt behaviour
BI = behavioural intention
$Aact$ = attitude towards the act
NB = normative belief
M_c = motivation to comply
and w_0, w_1 = empirically determined regression weights, and the following form when multiple reference groups are considered:

$$B \simeq BI = [Aact]w_0 + \left[\sum_{i=1}^{n} NB_i\,(M_{c_i})\right]w_1$$

A great deal of work has been concerned with respective correlations of the attitudinal and normative components of the model with behavioural intentions and of the way in which these components combine to produce measures of behavioural intentions. While this underlies the validation of the model and is thus of concern to all researchers, for applied social psychologists and those involved in investigations of consumer choice the crucial criterion of the model's usefulness is the ability of behavioural intentions to predict actual behaviour. Table 3.3 summarises a number of general studies in which $B1:B$ correlations have been reported. This table is based upon a survey of research presented by Ajzen and Fishbein[44] in 1973; more recently, success has been reported in the prediction of behaviour from behavioural intentions over a variety of different contexts. These include alcohol use,[45] voting on the building of nuclear power plants,[46] family planning,[47] and forces re-enlistment.[48] Table 3.4 summarises the results of four major published studies of the use of Fishbein's behavioural intentions model to predict purchase choice or related behaviour from intentions. The range of correlation coefficients among these studies is wide. They vary from 0.21 to 0.97 in the case of the general social psychological investigations mentioned in Table 3.3 and from 0.04 to 0.90 in the studies of consumer choice note in Table 3.4. (Full accounts of the assumptions and statistical procedures of analysis employed are available in the cited reports of the individual studies.) On the whole, however, the results of investigations employing the Fishbein formulation reflect the capacity to predict behaviour with a far higher degree of accuracy than is apparent from the studies of attitudinal–behavioural consistency reviewed by Wicker, where correlation coefficients rarely exceeded 0.30. The view was expressed earlier in this chapter that the improvement in correlations between prebehavioural factors (attitudes or intentions) and behaviour obtained subsequent to the revolution in attitude psychology which followed the inauguration of expectancy-value models and, in particular, multi-attribute models such as that of Fishbein, result from the incorporation of 'other (i.e. non-attitudinal) variables' into the prediction of behaviour.

The behavioural intentions model deliberately includes such 'other factors': Fishbein does not deny their indispensibility in the prediction of behavioural intentions or behaviour but asserts that their full effect is subsumed in the measured components of behavioural intentions, namely attitude towards the specified act and compliance with

58

Table 3.3 *BI: B correlations in social psychology**

Study	Intention	Correlation BI:B		N
Fishbein	Engage in pre-marital sexual intercourse	Males	0.394	21
		Females	0.676	14
		Total	0.447	35
Fishbein *et al.*	Lend communications to co-workers; comply with instructions of co-workers	Communication	0.690	144
		Compliance	0.211	144
Hornik	Maintain missiles in an experimental game	Grit	0.970	30
		RPM	0.858	30
		Hawk	0.521	30
		Total	0.867	90
Ajzen and Fishbein†	Intention to perform in Prisoner's Dilemma game	Co-operation	0.571	32
		Individualism	0.758	32
		Competition	0.765	32
		Total	0.897	96
Ajzen	Performance in PD game	Co-operation	0.578	36
		Competition	0.528	36
		Total	0.822	216
DeVries and Ajzen	Cheat in college	Copy from another	0.664	146
Darroch	Sign inter-racial photo release		0.462	107

* $p < 0.01$. Correlations, regression coefficients and multiple correlations of *Aact* and $NB(M_s)$ on *BI* are available in primary sources. See especially I. Ajzen and M. Fishbein, 'Attitudinal and Normative Variables as Predictors of Specific Behaviours', *Journal of Personality and Social Psychology*, vol. 27 (1973).

† Data refer to single game. Total refers to two similar games.

Sources: M. Fishbein, 'Sexual Behaviour and Propositional Control', *Proceedings of the Psychonomic Society*, 1966; M. Fishbein, I. Ajzen, E. Landy and L. R. Anderson, 'Attitudinal Variables and Behaviour' (Seattle, Washington: University of Washington, 1970); J. A. Hornik, 'Two Approaches to Individual Differences in an Expanded Prisoner's Dilemma Game', thesis (University of Illinois, 1970); I. Ajzen and M. Fishbein, 'The Prediction of Behaviour from Attitudinal and Normative Variables', *Journal of Experimental Social Psychology*, vol. 6 (1970) pp. 466–87; I. Ajzen, 'Attitudinal vs. Normative Messages', *Sociometry*, vol. 34 (1971) pp. 263–80; D. L. Devries and I. Ajzen, 'The Relationship of Attitudes and Normative Beliefs to Cheating in College', *Journal of Social Psychology*, vol. 83 (1971) pp. 199–207; R. K. Darroch, 'Attitudinal Variables and Perceived Group Norms as Predictors', thesis (University of Illinois, 1971).

Table 3.4 *BI:B correlations in consumer research*

Study	Intention	Correlation BI:B	N
Bonfield	Purchase of fruit drinks, various segments:		
	High importance	0.44^a	52
	Low importance	0.38^a	106
	High brand loyalty	0.04^a	53
	Medium brand loyalty	0.22	34
	Low brand loyalty	0.42^b	27
	Small household	0.42^b	90
	Large household	0.39^a	68
	Income < $10,000	0.32^a	102
	Income ≥ $10,000	0.56^a	56
	Low education	0.37^a	85
	High education	0.44^a	73
	Medium brand experience	0.41^a	93
	Wide brand experience	0.28	48
	Total sample	0.40^a	158
Harrel and Bennett	Physician prescribing specific brands of a drug		
	Brand A	0.52^a	93
	B	0.47^a	93
	C	0.27^a	93
	D	0.27^a	93
	E	0.34^a	93
Wilson, Matthews and Harvey	Purchase of specified toothpaste brand	0.90^a	162
Ryan and Bonfield	Application for loan at a credit union	0.33^a	93

* = p < 0.01.
† = p < 0.05.

Sources overleaf

Sources: E. H. Bonfield, 'Attitudes, Social Influence, Personal Norm and Intention Interactions as Related to Brand Purchase Behaviour', *Journal of Marketing Research*, vol. 11, no. 4 (1974) pp. 379–89; G. D. Harrel and P. D. Bennett, 'An Evaluation of the Expectancy Value Model of Attitude Measurement for Physician Prescribing Behaviour', *Journal of Marketing Research*, vol. 11, no. 4 (1974) pp. 269–78; D. T. Wilson, H. L. Mathews and J. W. Harvey, 'An Empirical Test of the Fishbein Behavioural Intentions Model', *Journal of Consumer Research*, vol. 1, no. 4 (1975) pp. 39–48; M. A. Ryan and E. H. Bonfield, 'The Fishbein Extended Model and Consumer Behaviour', *Journal of Consumer Research*, vol. 2, no. 2 (1975) pp. 118–36.

subjective norms. It is appropriate now to attempt to ascertain the extent to which the improvements in measured consistency are derived from the incorporation of non-attitudinal factors. The following discussion of this issue is conducted in the context of the studies of consumer choice to which reference has been made.

BI:B Consistency in Context

The Fishbein intentions model is presented by Ajzen and Fishbein as a device by which behaviour may be predicted from measures of behavioural intention, *only under certain very closely specified conditions*.[49] In short, the conditions in which measures of behavioural intention are obtained must be, 'maximally conducive to a high correlation between BI and B'.[50] High correlations are obtainable only when the period of time which intervenes between the measurement of the behavioural intention and that of the behavioural criterion is very short, when novel consequences of behaviour or reference group evaluations of the action under investigation do not intervene, when the behaviour is voluntary, and when the intention which accurately predicts behaviour is that which immediately precedes the act. The exogenous influences which invalidate more remote expressions of intention no doubt account for the equivocal capability of the Fishbein model to predict brand choice usefully in consumer research, that is in a manner which permits the rather long term forecasts required by marketing managers. The typical results summarised in Table 3.4 certainly give little encouragement to anyone involved in the attempt to reduce the extremely high failure rates of new consumer products.

The highest BI:B correlation (0.90) is that reported by Wilson, Matthews and Harvey, for their experiment in the prediction of the selection of brands of toothpaste from subjects' behavioural intentions: 85 per cent of the participants selected the brand regarding which they had expressed an intention to purchase.[51] The conditions appear to approximate closely those suggested by Ajzen and Fishbein as maximally conducive to a high correlation. Both responses involved precisely the same set of brands, the time lapse between the responses was short and the 'laboratory' situation and continued presence of the experimenter ensured close situational continuity. Although participants had responded to notices offering three dollars for their time and trouble, only two were paid in cash, the third being represented by a tube of toothpaste of approximately equivalent value. Opportunity for situational interventions to prompt deviation from the expressed intentions was thus minimal; indeed, the contingencies of reinforcement resulting from the presence of the experimenter during the overt brand choice almost certainly acted to ensure a high level of consistency between the verbal behaviour which was a response to the questionnaire based measurement of attitudes, norms and intentions, and the subsequent brand selection.

Schuman and Johnson evince scepticism about the usefulness of BI:B correlations obtained in laboratory settings, 'since they make little or no attempt to dissociate measurement of behavioural intention and measurement of behaviour, the extent to which consistency is evoked by the experimenter himself remains unknown. [Further] it is instructive to note that even in some of these idealised experiments, the correlations are surprisingly low.'[52] It would be mistaken to criticise Ajzen and Fishbein for the high levels of situational correspondence (and presumably contingencies of reinforcement) involved in the measurement of verbal and overt behaviour in laboratory investigations of the BI:B relationship: these conditions approximate well to those in which these authors argue their theory of reasoned action holds. What is important, however, is the avoidance of conclusions from such experimental work which ignore the many opportunities for situational interventions between the expression of purchase intentions in a consumer research setting and overt consumer choice behaviour at a later date in quite different circumstances and under new reinforcement contingencies.

Most instances of consumer research and subsequent consumer behaviour are clearly separated in time and circumstance by special offers, changes in income, product innovations, and so forth. As Ryan and Bonfield point out, many tests of the theory in the consumer domain have relied upon participants' self-reports as measures of behaviour or have employed laboratory type simulations which have not allowed temporal separation of the expression of behavioural intentions and the performance of the corresponding behaviour.[53] They might thus have constituted more exact tests of the theory of reasoned action as stated by its authors than some other investigations but the extrapolation of their results and conclusions to actual purchase situations is thereby unwarranted. High correlations between BI and B are not surprising in the circumstances of high situational correspondence advocated by Fishbein and Ajzen but because the behavioural measure in so many cases may be interpreted simply as a duplicate expression of intention, these investigations are less tests of Fishbein's model than measures of test-retest reliability.[54]

Many of the correlations obtained are much lower than 0.90, of course: the average discovered in one review of empirical investigations[55] was 0.435 and, in spite of the difficulties inherent in drawing conclusions from such averages, the implications for consumer research and marketing management appear unexciting. As has been noted, even investigators who have followed Fishbein and Ajzen's advice with respect to the necessity of ensuring close correspondence in the measurement of dependent and independent variables, have often produced low levels of measured consistency between BI and B. It is a commonplace procedure in non-laboratory studies to measure behaviour very soon after, concurrently with or prior to the measurement of intentions. In a survey based on the last of these, Harrel and Bennett obtained an average correlation of 0.40 between physicians' drug prescribing intentions for a patient and their actual prescriptions.[56] Intentions might well be a function of behaviour in such cases, a fact which is less a criticism of the investigators as a pointer to the origins of beliefs or self-reports obtained in studies of behavioural intentions. Several studies designed to recognise and incorporate situational intervention by using real world, consumer choice conditions as measures of behaviour, for example the investigations by Bonfield and Ryan and Bonfield, have, quite expectedly, produced low BI:B correlations.[57] The authors of the latter, which was concerned with identifying individuals who would make loan applications at a credit union, judge their results ($r = 0.33$, $p < 0.001$) to be encouraging in view of its avoidance of laboratory situations and the pencil and paper tests which might induce response set biases.

SITUATIONS AND BEHAVIOUR

Some Examples of Situational Influence

The recent history of research into the prediction of behaviour from 'attitudes' is actually the story of the inclusion of 'other variables' as factors which intervene between attitudes and behaviour. Before 1970 such factors were assumed by many social psychologists to account for the low recorded levels of attitudinal–behavioural consistency but little evidence of their effects existed; since then, however, extra-attitudinal influences have been made explicit in surveys of attitudes and behaviour and Wicker's assertion that, 'In studies in which extraneous events can intervene to disrupt the relationship between intentions and acts, judgements of the influence of such events may improve the prediction of behaviour'[58] has been taken more and more seriously. If consumer researchers have not succeeded in isolating the precise effects of situational influences upon attitudinal–behavioural relationships, it has at least become normal to show an appreciation of the situational vicissitudes which may account for the empirical demonstration of inconsistency or low levels of consistency. Physicians' prescription of a given brand of drug might reflect, for instance, prescribing practice for other patients, the initial prescribing decision of a doctor who had previously treated a patient, patients' reactions to particular drugs and brands, government studies of the side effects of specific brands, recent influence of commercial information sources such as sales representatives or advertisements in the medical press, and information from colleagues. These are factors mentioned by Harrell and Bennett as potential situational modifiers.

Harrell and Bennett's examples are, of course, taken from the context of a single study. Although the impact of situational influences upon consumer choice will be dealt with in greater detail in the following chapter, it may be worthwhile to clarify the nature and effect of situational interventions at this point, particularly in order that they may be distinguished from attitudinal factors. In his account of a meta-theoretical framework for the study of economic behaviour, van Raaij recognises that, 'Behavioural intentions lead to behaviour if no anticipated or unanticipated situations arise and prevent the realisation of the behavioural intentions.'[59] This is in agreement with the theme of this chapter. He goes on to specify the sorts of intervention to which he is referring:

These situations may be emergencies, accidents, illness, a bank refusing credit, sudden unemployment, marriage, birth of a child. The longer the time lag between behavioural intention and actual behaviour, the higher the possibility of situational interventions. Economic behaviour is also influenced by anticipated situations: a party, a weekend trip, being with your partner. Consumers tend to differentiate their product [brand, or store] selection according to anticipated usage situations.[60]

The result for theory of this move towards the explication of consumer choice behaviour in situational and other non-attitudinal as well as attitudinal terms has been a move away from the simple notion of attitudinal–behavioural consistency. Rokeach probably originated the giving of importance to the situationally prescribed measurement of attitudes and behaviour in place of 'attitude towards the object' through his insistence on paying close attention to 'attitude towards the situation'.[61] The encouraging results of Fishbein and Ajzen derive not only from the constraints they place upon the definition and measurement of attitude and behaviour but from their freedom from a restrictive search for narrow attitudinal–behavioural consistency. Fishbein repeatedly emphasises this in a paper written expressly for consumer researchers which is, nevertheless, often overlooked in accounts of attitudes and behaviour in the context of consumer choice.[62] After reviewing the results of a number of prisoners' dilemma experiments, he spells out that the findings:

clearly indicate that even when appropriate attitudes are considered (i.e. attitudes towards the performance of a behaviour rather than attitudes towards an object or person) a change in that attitude may not produce behavioural change and thus even under these conditions (i.e. when appropriate attitudes are considered) there is little reason to expect attitudinal-behavioural consistency . . . clearly the time has come to stop worrying about consistency and to start worrying about those factors that control behaviour.[63]

According to the theory of reasoned action, those attitudinal factors which prefigure and control behaviour are themselves highly specific to given situations. Non–attitudinal factors which control behaviour are taken into account by the two major determinants of behavioural intention which constitute the independent variables of the behavioural intentions model, and do not require additional measurement or incorporation in the regression equations shown earlier. Thus all of the determinants of behavioural intention and, therefore, of the behaviour it is assumed to approximate are situationally modified; the relative importance of attitude towards the act and subjective norm in any given instance of behavioural prediction is determined by the nature of the behaviour in question, the contextual conditions specified for its performance and the personal characteristics of the individual. (The measurement of these separately specified components may well include both attitudinal and normative determinants according to Miniard and Cohen;[64] if so, their correct specification should be as interactive variables rather than independent explicators of behavioural intention and hence multiplicative rather than additive.)

Situations and Intentions

The problem for consumer researchers who are concerned with the production of consumer choice is that the Fishbein behavioural intentions model and its accompanying theory of reasoned action do not take situational factors sufficiently into account for their purposes. Fishbein and Ajzen follow Dulany in regarding behavioural intentions as the immediate antecedents of behaviour but it is generally impossible or of negligible practical significance in consumer research to measure behavioural intentions at so late a stage in the buying process. In positive recognition of this, Sheth makes explicit the fact of the respondent's expectation and anticipation of novel situational contexts at the time of behaviour.[65] He hypothesises the determinants of behavioural intentions thus:

$$BI_{ij} = b_1 (EB_{ijk}) + b_2 (SE_{ij}) + b_3 (AS_{ij})$$

where BI_{ij} = individual i's plan to act in a particular way towards object j

EB_{ijk} = individual i's evaluative belief k about object j

SE_{ij} = individual i's social environment as it impinges upon his behaviour towards j

AS_{ij} = individual i's expectation and anticipation of events at the time of his behaviour towards j

and b_1, b_2, b_3 = regression weights.

The social environment comprises those elements of the situation in which behaviour occurs which are the source of the individual's social norms. It must be determined separately for each research situation. This is borne out by the considerable body of knowledge in sociology and social psychology which demonstrates that reference group influences have both a moderating effect upon attitudinal factors and an independent effect upon the control of behaviour. The anticipated situation comprises 'all the other activities that the individual is likely to engage in at the time of future behaviour as he perceives and forecasts them now and when expressing his plan or intention to behave'.[66] Although the components of this anticipated situation also vary, Sheth notes the following general factors, '(1) cyclical phenomena such as holidays, vacations, birthdays, schooling and education; (2) anticipated mobility (since mobility is very prevalent and increasing, a number of buying decisions may be strictly due to this factor); and (3) financial status of the decision-maker, including anticipated incomes and expenditures'.[67] Engel, Blackwell and Kollat list such 'anticipated circumstances' as financial status, availability of goods, access to retail outlets and general optimism or pessimism about the economy which may affect intentions, and they advocate the inclusion of these influences in models of behavioural intentions in addition to the attitudinal and normative elements used by Fishbein.[68]

Consumer choice is not, however, simply a function of expressed behavioural intentions; since most consumer research into intentions precedes behaviour by days, weeks or even months, that behaviour is also a function of unpredictable situational interventions. Although, in Sheth's words it is theoretically possible to, 'produce a very high positive correlation between Behavioural Intention and actual behaviour if the two are measured contiguously in time and space, because then we allow no freedom for outside factors to intervene and mediate'[69] actual consumer research and consumer behaviour do not occur contiguously and behaviour is controlled to some degree by unexpected events. Thus:

$$B_{ijt} = b_1 \left(A_{ij,t-n} \right) + b_2 \left(BI_{ij,t-n} \right) + b_3 \left(UE_{ijt} \right)$$

where B_{ijt} = a specific behaviour performed by individual i at time t towards object j

$A_{ij,t-n}$ = affect towards the object expressed at time t-n

$BI_{ij,t-n}$ = individual i's intention to behave in a certain manner towards object j as expressed at time t-n

UE_{ijt} = unexpected events which impinge upon individual i's behaviour at time t towards object j.

and b_1, b_2, b_3 = regression weights.

Sheth attributes the inability of social psychologists and consumer researchers to demonstrate attitudinal–behavioural consistently to unexpected events. 'It is my contention', he writes, 'that the influence of Unexpected Events is very much under-represented in studies of buying behaviour because of our zeal to give a rational explanation for all behaviour. In other words, we have based our thinking on the assumption that all buying decisions are intentional behaviour.'[70] All of these considerations give substance to the essential problem of employing behavioural intentions models in consumer research: purchase intentions are likely to remain inchoate until an opportunity to behave presents itself.[71]

Intentions and Beliefs

Sheth's own empirical research testing of this model and that of other researchers such as Bearden and Woodside[72] adds weight to the view that situational 'other variables' are of paramount importance in the explanation, though not necessarily as yet the prediction, of consumer behaviour. Yet the beliefs, of which the two major components of Fishbein's intentions model and the model of affect which underlies Sheth's hypothesis are composed, cannot be ignored. Are beliefs and behavioural intentions cognitive elements, mental determinants of behaviour or are they the verbal self-reports of individuals who are describing their past experience?

Ehrenberg and Goodhardt emphatically assert that their measures of behavioural intention accurately reflect past buying behaviour and could be better termed measures of behavioural usage.[73] Their work over a wide range of conditions has established the empirical relationship:

$$I = \sqrt{K / U}$$

where I = intentions to buy (and is taken to be the consumer's overall evaluation of the brand)

U = usage level (per cent using the brand)

and K = a constant (which is identical for each brand within a product class but varies from product to product)

These authors argue that:

A consumer's overall attitude to a brand may be summarised by her expressed intention to buy the brand. For brands of frequently-bought products, expressed intentions to buy are closely related to consumers' usage behaviour. The intention-to-buy variable is in fact a measure of past buying behaviour and not a prediction of future buying, especially not of *changes* in buying behaviour.[74]

The implication of this is not that verbal statements of behavioural intention, affect or overall evaluation derive from an underlying, 'true' attitude which mediates both this verbal expression of opinion and subsequent overt behaviour, but that the verbal statement of intention is a form of behaviour itself, one which is highly contingent upon prior overt behaviour and its consequences. The verbal behaviour of which statements of attitude or intention are composed can be expected to show consistency with future overt behaviour only if similar circumstances and contingencies of reinforcement govern both. This explanation of verbal behaviour does not posit intervening latent processes but concentrates directly upon behaviour as a function of behaviour. As DeFleur and Westie put it, 'A latent something interposed between attitudinal behaviour patterns and the social variables which mediate them is simply unnecessary.'[75]

Thus Ehrenberg and Goodhardt explain apparent inconsistencies between intentions and purchase and between usage and purchase not in terms of mediating, 'psychological' states but in terms of the indefinite time period to which intentions to buy relate while usage data refer to a specified past period of time. The tendency of verbalised intentions to be reports on previous and current experience is evident from the fact that:

> almost all 'current' users of the brand say they intend to buy it. This makes sense – they are using it currently [presumably with positive reinforcements], and mostly say that they intend to go on buying it. But otherwise the level of intention-to-buy decreases with degree of past usage, from almost 50 per cent among those who have used the brand in the last 6 months, to 10 per cent among those who have tried it while not currently using it, and 5 per cent among those who have not tried it.[76]

Attitudes from Behaviour

There are good grounds, therefore, for holding the view that the verbal behaviour labelled 'attitude' in social science research tends to follow avert behaviour rather than precede it, even though verbal expressions of 'opinion' (i.e. past experience and its consequences) is part of the situational context of future behaviour and thus guides it. Fishbein's reasoning is consistent with this in that, 'although an individual's attitude might initially influence and be related to specific behavioural intentions (or to specific behaviours), this relationship may or may not persist, depending on the nature and schedule of reinforcement associated with the behavioural intentions.'[77] Cognitive psychologists have long been aware of the behaviour → attitude sequence and the most popular explanation of this 'revised sequence' proceeds in terms of Festinger's theory of cognitive dissonance reduction.[78] An example of this reduction process would be an individual changing his attitudes to match his behaviour after behaving in a way that was inconsistent with them. A more complete explanation of these phenomena is put forward by Bem, a radical behaviourist much influenced by Skinner's account of verbal learning.[79] This is the theory of self-perception according to which attitudes are inferred by an individual from his own observations of his own behaviour, much as others draw inferences about his likes and dislikes from their observations. Those verbalised observations which constitute an individual's attitudes may act as self-instructions which help shape subsequent behaviour.

While more will be said about Bem's theory in Chapter 4, it is worthwhile noting here that there is a great deal of evidence in social psychology generally to support this view, from the finding that relevant past behaviour can account significantly for variance in present behaviour without resort to the mediation of behavioural intentions as an explicative device,[80] to the contention of Triandis that habit rather than verbally expressed intention provides the more reliable guide to future behaviour.[81] A major study of blood donation reported by Bagozzi draws upon behavioural learning theory to explain the finding that:

at least for novel, costly behaviours such as the donation of blood, the formation of an expectancy-value attitude in memory appears to be contingent on prior experience with the focal attitudinal act. This was dramatically shown in the analyses wherein it was found that those who had never given blood failed to possess valid expectancy-value attitudes while those who had given blood did form valid expectancy-value attitudes.[82]

This is, moreover, entirely consistent with Fishbein and Ajzen's account of the formation and modification of beliefs – which are the building blocks of the components of behavioural intention – through experience, reinforcement and the recall of contingencies and consequences.[83] In the study of consumer choice, the further implication is that whether measures of intention constitute trustworthy indicators of behaviour depends upon the coincidence of identical contingencies of reinforcement in the situations in which the verbal expression of intention occurs (and thus reflect the individual's reinforcement history). Engel, Blackwell and Kollat's advocacy of the inclusion of a further situational variable in the intentions model thus receives additional support since the expression of 'anticipated circumstances' undoubtedly reflects experience and thus links past and future situation based contingencies.

The addition of situational variables to models of attitude and behaviour appears to be a means of assessing the extent to which present and future contingencies coincide and thus of the extent to which verbal and overt behaviours will match. The theory of propositional control devised by Dulany,[84] which is the antecedent of Fishbein's behaviour intentions model, certainly suggests this behaviourist interpretation:

$$BI = [[RHd)(A)]w_o + [(BH)(M_c)]w_1$$

where $BI =$ the intention of the individual to respond in a particular way

$RHd =$ a 'hypothesis of the distribution of reinforcement', i.e. the individual's theory that this response will have particular consequences

$A =$ the affective value of the reinforcement

$BH =$ behavioural hypothesis

$M_c =$ motivation to comply

$w_o, w_1 =$ regression weights.

The interpretation suggested if 'verbal behaviour' is substituted for 'cognitions', 'affect' and 'attitude' in accounts of overt behaviour and its prediction.

The link between situational specificity and the tenets of the behaviourist paradigm is also apparent for the observation that of 'other variables' listed by Wicker:

the expected and/or actual consequences of various acts may be the most fundamental of the situational factors . . . since most of the others can be subsumed within it. For example, it can be argued that the presence or absence of certain people, and norms prescribing proper behaviour are ones which help to define the contingencies in a particular situation . . . Also it may be that the more similar the stimuli to which verbal and overt behaviour responses are made, the most likely it is that the same contingencies will exist for a favourable or an unfavourable response and thus consistency would result.[85]

SUMMARY AND CONCLUSION

Attitude is most frequently defined in both social psychology and consumer research in terms which derive from latent process conceptions of this construct. Thus attitude is generally depicted in terms of intervening mental or hypothetical concepts which determine behaviour regardless of its situational context. Behaviour is represented as the result of attitudes which are, in turn, the output of intrapersonal information processing. Latent process conceptions belong to the cognitive psychological paradigm and, consistent with this, models of consumer decision making portray consumer choice as a function of attitudinal dynamics which stem largely from 'persuasive marketing'. Evidence for the consistency of measures of attitude and behaviour upon which latent process definitions of attitude are posited is extremely weak and it is only when situational variables are added that the prediction of behaviour becomes reliable. Even the strongest proponents of latent process conceptions recognise the effects of non-attitudinal influences on behaviour, thereby weakening considerably the notion of an underlying, 'true' attitude which mediates both verbal and overt behaviour regardless of environment. At the least, therefore, the prevailing consumer research paradigm which rests upon the major assumptions of cognitive information processing psychology must be brought up to date by recognizing the necessity of attaching far greater explicative significance to situational factors. At the most, the argument that a behaviourist paradigm for consumer research provides a legitimate alternative to cognitive psychology now rests upon a body of empirical knowledge and reasoning which is difficult to ignore.

By concentrating upon the construct of attitude, this chapter has dealt with the central component of consumer psychology. In order to clarify the paradigmatic implications of the argument pursued, it is necessary to consider more generally the nature of consumer research and marketing management and the significance for these practices of a paradigm shift.

Chapter 4

Directions and Developments in Consumer Research

PARADIGM SHIFT?

The conclusions reached in Chapter 3 relate strictly to a single, albeit central, construct. Because attitude has so long dominated consumer research any suggestion that it should be radically reconceptualised naturally carries paradigmatic implications but is not of itself sufficient to provoke a paradigm shift. Rather, the implication is that the cognitive information processing paradigm be subjected to greater critical appraisal than is currently the case. The conclusions of the last chapter deviate from those of many, perhaps most, social psychologists and consumer researchers. This difference is not about principles, for even the most ardent exponents of the latent process view now accept many qualifications forced upon them by the operational research generated by the 'other variables' approach. Rather, the difference lies in the general failure of behavioural scientists, especially those involved in consumer research, to make explicit the inadvisability of further search for attitudinal–behavioural consistency and to accept that the evidence on attitudinal–behavioural inconsistency is sufficiently far reaching to make necessary a more general re-examination of the prevailing paradigm within which they work.

At most, the evidence would encourage the adoption of a behaviourist paradigm as one of a number of competing paradigms in consumer research. This need not necessarily be the radical behaviourism described earlier. They could well adopt the less extreme behavioural learning theories which have not placed the locus of control entirely outside of the individual. At least, the conclusions reached in Chapter 3 confirm the need for a more explicit questioning of the dominant paradigm. Perhaps some form of reconstruction of that framework is under way already as researchers increasingly allude to the 'complexities' of the results of investigations of consumer information processing while others turn more and more to consider the situational and other contextual factors which constitute the environment of consumer choice. It is also possible that a middle way will emerge, a framework which is not merely eclectic but which convincingly integrates elements of cognitive and behaviourist approaches.[1]

Any of these is possible since there is already mention of behaviourist and integrated approaches, as well as of the cognitive information processing framework, in the literature of consumer behaviour. Indeed, the eclecticism of the consumer research discipline has been one of its strengths, encouraging researchers to avoid the internal debates of the parent behavioural science disciplines and to concentrate upon the transfer of concepts and methods which are significant for marketing. But, if the response to the recent call for a behaviourist perspective in consumer research made by Kassarjian[2] merely reflects the openness of marketing scholars to new perspectives without considering the wider implications of confirming so radical a framework of conception and analysis, then the very eclecticism which has been of immense assistance to the development of academic consumer research over the past twenty years may serve only to inhibit further progress. Any call for a comprehensive paradigm shift would be unjustified and forecasts of radical paradigmatic change are certainly premature. But the problem of attitudinal–behavioural inconsistency will not disappear and demands an adequate response.

As was pointed out in Chapter 1, this response may necessitate far reaching reformulation rather than mere technical development. Even the most mature science is beset by conceptual and methodological difficulties: they are part of the pursuit of 'normal science' and do not have revolutionary consequences. But the near phrenetic attempts to 'explain' the empirical data of consumer research within implicit perspectives and the proliferation of techniques capable of generating and preparing those data are indicative of a science in crisis rather than in progress. The discussion which follows is addressed to some of the issues which require attention in the course of a more comprehensive assessment of the prevailing paradigm within which consumer research is executed and its alternative. The purpose of this discussion is to allow readers to judge – not only from the author's conclusions but from subsequent, first hand evaluation of the primary sources – the extent to which an alternative approach to consumer choice is supported by empirical research findings and their interpretation and how far leading consumer researchers are themselves becoming critical of the dominant paradigm, cognitive information processing.

Three broad themes are evident in the following discussion of the model of consumer behaviour, its nature and determinants, which figures prominently in current consumer research. The notion of consumers' prebehavioural decision processes is coterminous with information processing approaches; but consumer researchers are becoming increasingly aware of the situational influences which impinge upon consumer choice; and a few have conducted research which is concerned with the direct modification of choice behaviour.

CONSUMER DECISION-MAKING

The pervasive belief among marketing researchers that consumer choice is rational and intentional was encountered in the previous chapter. For some years it has formed the basis of the process in which models of consumer behaviour have been developed and tested.

Consumer researchers, like their cousins in cognate areas of behavioural investigation, have rejected the microeconomic model in their work precisely because its assumption of perfect knowledge obviates decision making and thus choice. The models which they have devised typically involve the cognitive decision sequence which includes the problem specification, search for and comparative evaluation of solutions and their consequences, deciding and choosing. This is the sequence posited by the information processing models of consumer choice considered in Chapter 1. The volumes of research generated within this framework stem from studies of every phase of the postulated decision making sequence and the cognitive processes assumed to accompany them. In addition to the specification and testing of multi-attribute models[3] and the prediction of brand choice on the basis of measures of beliefs, and intentions[4] which were noted in Chapter 2, this research has taken the form of investigations of the modification of attitudes through prior cognitive change,[5] the effects upon attitudes and intentions of informative (or persuasive) communication,[6] decision making under conditions of uncertainty,[7] the direction of causal relations among perceptions, cognitions, affect, behavioural intentions and behaviour,[8] and the processing and recall of information.[9] Each of these areas of research is, however, characterised by debate and controversy including severe disagreements over the interpretation of results and the validity of research instruments. The task of critical consumer researchers is to judge whether this can be safely accounted for as the inevitable 'creative conflict' inherent within any healthily developing discipline or whether it is indicative of the need for a radically rethought approach. While it is not possible to review all of the recent literature here, the following discussion is intended to be illustrative of current issues.

Cognition, Attitude and Behaviour

Some of the earliest research directed towards the validation of multi-attribute models such as that of Fishbein for further use in consumer research was carried out by Tuck,[10] who draws attention to the need to ensure that measures of belief refer to usage when attitude towards acts of usage are under investigaton.[11] Her work, she notes, justifies Fishbein's own argument that 'attitude to a brand must be distinguished from attitude to using that brand in a specific context, which in turn must be distinguished from intention to use that brand which in turn may differ from observed behaviour *vis-à-vis* that brand.'[12] This in itself reinforces the need to take situation specific measurements of attitudes and behaviour. Several studies carried out in the United States have consisted of tests of the sequence of effects postulated by the full behavioural intentions model. Lutz has reported several investigations of the causal relationship between the cognitive, affective and conative elements of the extended Fishbein model.[13] In contradistinction to most European research, he used a hypothetical brand and attitudes were measured in a laboratory context. Although some evidence of the effect of cognitive change on attitudinal change was found, Lutz concludes that, 'from a managerial perspective, the weakness of the relationship between cognitive change and attitudinal change is disturbing'.[14] Yet he concludes also that for marketing theorists, the results are encouraging because they confirm the hierarchy of effects idea.

Lutz's conclusions and methods have, however, been criticised and qualified by a number of fellow researchers. Dickson and Miniard point out that the sequence in which attitudes follow behaviour is confirmed by both empirical investigation and theoretical reasoning.[15] Within the sphere of cognitive psychology, Festinger's theory of dissonance reduction is an attempt to explain post decisional changes in beliefs or attitudes;[16] Krugman argues that where individual involvement is low, attitude formation and change will be negligible prior to action;[17] and, among behaviourists, the self-attribution theory devised by Bem which casts verbal (or attitudinal) behaviour as reports of previous behaviour, is clearly consistent with this.[18] 'Consequently', Dickson and Miniard conclude, 'one may posit a configuration with an opposite flow of causation [from that] hypothesised by the Fishbein Model.'[19] Lutz's response to this recognises the existence of two paradigms of attitudinal–behavioural relationships and causation and emphasises that his investigation was undertaken with in the attitude →behaviour framework and the results must be judged accordingly.[20]

In research which appears not to be hampered by theoretical assumptions, Ginter concludes that both pre-purchase and post-purchase attitude change occurs but that the latter is of greater magnitude.[21] Post purchase change in attitude is, moreover, the more highly correlated with consumer choice. Corroborative results and conclusions were reported by Reibstein, Lovelock and Dobson on the basis of their investigation of travel behaviour: 'Perceptions influenced, and were influenced by, behaviour as long as these beliefs led to affect and affect led to behaviour. When affect was deleted from the relationships, beliefs were influenced by behaviour, but not vice versa.'[22] Recent investigations reported by Bagozzi find that the relationship of attitude on intention may be small. Furthermore, 'when the extent of past behaviour is taken into account, the influence of attitude is reduced still further, although its effect is statistically significant. In sum, attitude does appear to influence behaviour, but its impact is a relatively small one.'[23] Past behaviour also appears to affect the intentions → behaviour relationship since, 'as habit increases, the performance of the behaviour becomes less one of a rational evaluation of the consequences of the act and more one of a learned response.'[24] Bagozzi infers that attitudes and intentions may correspond not only in terms of the four dimensions proposed by Fishbein and Ajzen (action, target, context and time) but in terms of the act's *consequences*.

Even so cursory a survey of recent research into attitudinal and behavioural dynamics conducted by consumer researchers indicates a field in some disarray. It appears that results with respect to the directionality of attitudinal–behavioural effects depend upon what the investigator wishes to demonstrate. No superordinate research framework permits a final conclusion to be reached with respect to the direction of attitude–behaviour links, nor is there any convincing explanation of why attitude change may on some occasions precede behaviour and on others follow it. The results gathered in this research programme are, as reflection shows, explicable in terms of the behaviourist paradigm, though the reader must judge whether behaviourism offers a more convincing or more managerially useful account. At the very least, however, the results suggest that conventional explanations of consumer decision making which proceed in terms of a hierarchy of information processing effects must be subjected to greater critical evaluation than his hitherto been the case. Does research which has been concerned directly with the capacity of consumers to process information confirm this?

Information Processing

The hypothesised relationship between exposure to information and subsequent intrapersonal data processing which ends in action posited by hierarchy of effects models was thoroughly tested in a series of investigations undertaken during the 1970s, notably by Jacoby[25] and Bettman.[26] (Incidentally the results of this research further disconfirm the pattern of attitudinal–behavioural consistency commonly assumed in the marketing literature.) Investigations of consumers' reactions to the enhanced provision of nutritional information on the labels of food products led to the conclusion that, *'the vast majority of consumers neither use nor comprehend nutrition information in arriving at food purchase decisions'.*[27] This finding weakens effect hierarchy/information processing approaches; it also suggests that the provisions of such models are no longer taken for granted by many consumer researchers who are now asking for evidence that consumers understand information to which they are exposed and that they make use of it. Earlier experimentation by Jacoby, Speller and Kohn indicated that the provision of increased amounts of information led consumers to report verbally on their greater satisfaction and reduced confusion but was followed by their making less rational purchase choices.[28] The study is, of course, subject to the limitations of any social experiment but its authors contend that it resembles closely the situation in which a customer beginning to purchase from an established product class finds himself. In such circumstances, they conclude, the customer's evoked set is relatively small and choice within it is based upon the most salient three to five product attributes rather than upon the totality of information available.

This research does not provide evidence that consumers make no use of information before buying but it casts strong doubt upon the hypothesised pattern of consumer information processing which has been prevalent in consumer research and in marketing management and education. The importance of previous purchase and consumption experience is increasingly recognised in these and related studies[29] and facilitates the explanation of consumers' behaviour in terms of their overtly accessible reinforcement histories rather than their covert information processing. Such results as these have not gone unchallenged (for example, Scammon[30]) but are representative of the growing basis for dissatisfaction among consumer researchers with the conventional wisdom of the information processing model.

Concomitant research has raised such issues as the design of consumer information environments,[31] the format in which information is presented and its relationship with consumers' data processing,[32] information processing in situations of varying task complexity,[33] and motivational aspects of processing.[34] The difficulties unearthed by recent research into consumers' comprehension and use of information may not have weakened the hold of the cognitive information processing paradigm on leading consumer researchers, but their results and conclusions provide grounds for an alternative approach. Furthermore, many of the findings of consumer researchers who work within this paradigm do not find an obvious interpretation even within so well developed a framework. For instance, the finding that consumers' use of information on product labels most frequently revolves around brand name and price while much additional data are largely ignored is shown by Jacoby, Szybillo and Busato-Schach to be open to at least four interpretations.[35] First, it may imply the 'chunking' of information, a phenomenon in which several types of information are grouped together into units so that the presentation of a single piece of information may convey a number of other product or brand characteristics. Secondly, recollection of a brand name might have led potential buyers to believe that their knowledge of the brand in question exceeded their knowledge of alternatives; they would, therefore, not seek further information about familiar brands. Thirdly, when brand names were not made available (condition of the research) the novelty of the situation might have prompted search. And, finally, the non-availability of some brand names might have stimulated rational information search. The authors do not consider the possibility that customers might have discriminated on the basis of their reinforcement histories; the consequences of purchasing novel brands in the absence of information from reinforcing sources might well be instrumental in shaping their search behaviour during the experiment.

Although the authors of this interesting investigation clearly favour the 'chunking' hypothesis, they show an undogmatic approach to the interpretation of their data, albeit one which does not extend beyond the cognitive information processing paradigm. To do so would be to propose that consumer decision making is less central to the explanation and prediction of consumer choice than has been almost universally believed in the marketing research community. Few have dissented from this widespread belief though Olshavsky and Granbois are among those who have argued convincingly that the notion of universal consumer decision making must be re-examined:

> A significant proportion of purchases may not be preceded by a decision process. This conclusion does not simply restate the familiar observation that purchase behaviour rapidly becomes habitual, with little or no prepurchase processes occurring after the first few processes. We conclude that for many purchases a decision process never occurs, not even on the first purchase.[36]

'Search → Evaluation → Choice'

Systematic problem solving, even within what Simon calls 'bounded rationality',[37] involves at relatively early stages a *search* for alternative courses of action. In the consumer field this is usually presented as the identification of as many potentially problem solving items (products, brands, stores and so on) as possible. While it is recognised that search incurs costs, economic, social and psychological[38], the rational models of consumer choice are posited on more rather than less external investigation. Yet it is well known that decision making or choice in consumer behaviour, industrial buying behaviour and organisational problem solving generally is often preceded by consideration of only two or three possibilities and that the persual of a single outcome is frequently encountered.[39]

Granbois reports that, for a significant range of household purchases, only one retail outlet is visited prior to purchase: 75–80 per cent of soft goods are purchased in this way: 50 per cent of buyers of colour television sets, 39 per cent of monochrome television set buyers, 27 per cent of buyers of carpets and 22 per cent of furniture purchasers report a single store visit.[40] In several surveys of purchases of consumer durables, between 10 and 71 per cent of buyers are reported as using a single pre-purchase source of information, a single price range, or a single brand. A majority of respondents in other investigations report using little or no such data.[41] Often in-store communication sources (e.g. salesmen, point of sale advertising) are the sole channels of information; in-store deliberation or problem solving appears absent from consumers' behaviour; and impulse buying provides the only explanation of choice.[42] Interpersonal, reference group influence, including personal recommendation appears to take the place of the assumed information search in many cases. The behavioural influence of situational factors such as the physical arrangement of store interiors (e.g. shelf height) replaces the imputed identification of a base set of alternative brands; and proxy, summary measures of quality such as price, brand names and packaging familiarity are substituted for the posited search for information capable of forming the basis of rational evaluation and comparison.[43] Learned responses acquired in the process of consumer socialisation appear more determinative than cognitively based deliberation.[44]

The comparative *evaluation* of possible solutions is a common theme of models of rational or quasi-rational problem solving and decision making. Thompson states that, 'decision issues always involve two major dimensions: (1) beliefs about cause/effect relationships and (2) preferences regarding possible outcomes'.[44] The widespread assumption of quasi-rational decision making in the consumer behaviour literature is based upon the notion that customers have the capacity to process large amounts of information and that they do so. The preceding discussion indicates that they often neither seek such information on anywhere near so large a scale as has been claimed nor do they use it. Rather the evidence leads to the conclusion that consumers reduce the risk (probability) of aversive consequences by considering fewer options rather than more and that comparatively little information is actually employed in the prepurchase stages of behaviour. Subjective opportunity costs are seldom estimated in any sense. Yet the consumers whose purchasing behaviour has been discussed in this book and the researchers who have investigated it are inhabitants of societies which value the idea of rational action. It is also to be noted that investigations of consumer choice which attempt to gain access to buyers' mental processes by requiring them to make verbal statements describing their actions as they take place cannot avoid respondents' self-ascription of rationality.

The idea that behaviour is purposeful and intentional is especially appealing but post behavioural 'explanations' of choice in terms of supposed pre-behavioural objectives are difficult to interpret. Such verbalisations and the 'verbal protocols' (word for word compilations of contemporary thought processes[45]) gained in behavioural process research are instantly reinforced by the research situation or have been positively reinforced so frequently that they are an unreliable guide to present covert behaviour and offer only poor approximations to subsequent behaviour. 'The objectives' writes Brunsson, 'are arguments, not criteria for choice.'[46] There is little attempt, if any, to reduce uncertainty by the acquisition of information which transforms it into some subjective notion of risk, that is the attachment of probabilities to outcomes. Rather risk is avoided and uncertainty managed by the minimal prebehavioural consideration of more than one outcome.

It is also apparent from the multiplicity of multi-attribute attitude models and means of measuring and combining their components that researchers are far from agreed about the strategy used by consumers in assessing attributes and brands. (Compare for example the summative Fishbein behavioural intentions model with that of Sheth as presented in Chapter 3.) Engel, Blackwell and Kollat discuss a number of models which imply different approaches to judgement and evaluation on the part of consumers (compensatory models of the expectancy-value and attribute adequacy variety; non-compensatory models of the conjunctive, disjunctive and lexicographic types) and they conclude somewhat equivocally that 'It is likely that any of the above methods will be used by consumers in certain circumstances, and the evidence seems to confirm that this indeed is the case.'[47] Controversy has been particularly evident over whether evaluative responses should be summated or averaged and the assumption of one or other has crucial implications for marketing practice.[48]

Finally, *choice* is expected to be the outcome of the search and evaluation process, although there is little evidence that consumers in general plan their financial allocations in order that criteria by which the various options can be judged can be developed on a systematic basis.[49] From their review Olshavsky and Granbois conclude that, 'perhaps one fourth to one third of all consumers show evidence of systematic planning and decision-making regarding saving; the majority, however, may not be classified as deliberate choosers.'[50] Even so-called discretionary income, they state, is not allocated with genuine discretion: social and situational factors exert shaping influences which are of paramount importance. Information search behaviour varies with social class for both consumer durables and non-durables[51] and it is reasonable to conclude that interpersonal pressures often preclude deliberation and choice in the sense of conscious selection among alternatives.

Even if cognitive decision making were a definable measureable entity, the diverse effects of situational intervention between the making and verbal expression of a decision and the opportunity for overt behavioural choice, which was demonstrated in Chapter 3, renders predictions of consumer choice of dubious worth. Overall, consumers do not appear to use the large amounts of information which the rational decision making models advance as the central feature of consumer choice. The probability is that it is more predictable from social pressures, 'culturally mandated life-styles' and other situational variables than from attempts to penetrate the intrapersonal framework of information processing.

Attitudinal-Behavioural Dynamics

It is interesting to note that some writers on marketing who have examined attitudinal-behavioural dynamics in some depth have moved towards this position. Pinson and Roberto are among them.[52] They begin by citing a number of marketing academics and practitioners for whom the proposition that attitudinal change necessarily precedes behavioural change is obvious.

> It is difficult to conceive of a change in behaviour occurring without some prior change in the organism . . . some attitude change must precede behavioural change barring the circumstances of coercion. Some internal change must precede a new external act assuming that that act is voluntary . . . The natural feeling of those in the advertising business that attitude changes must precede changes in behaviour must be tautologically true unless, for example, people buy things which, at least at the time of purchase, they dislike.[53]

Pinson and Roberto subsequently point out that the idea that attitudinal change is a necessary antecedent of behavioural change is untenable even among cognitive psychologists unless the concept of attitude is so defined as to subsume all internal states such as self-concepts, personality, and those attributable to physiological events. Perhaps early psychologists understood 'attitude' in such general terms but scientific progress has certainly set close bounds to its definition. These authors do not reject the cognitive approach; they accept the proposition that some internal psychological change almost certainly precedes behavioural response, whether or not coercion is present, but do not find that the internal process must necessarily be defined in terms of 'attitude' as that construct is nowadays understood. Furthermore, if attitudinal–behavioural consistency is understood to mean that behaviour is invariably preceded by an approprite behavioural predisposition, liking, or set of beliefs, then it is a tautological proposition which is unlikely to be of practical use in most contexts. They argue that any causal relationship between attitudes and actions is situation specific and that the task of consumer researchers is now to determine under which particular circumstances – social, economic, psychological – attitudes precede behaviour.

One way out of the tautology of attitudinal–behavioural consistency which arises from the assertion that behaviour is necessarily preeded by attitudes arises from the observation that attitudinal change (or, at least, a change in verbal behaviour) *follows* behavioural change. The theory of cognitive dissonance advanced by Festinger[54] does not avoid such phenomena as a consumer's increased liking for a product after he has bought it: rather, the assumed process of dissonance reduction in which the individual brings his attitudes into line with his prior behaviour is the very substance of this approach which has had a strong impact upon marketing thought and advertising practice. In spite of the controversy which still surrounds dissonance theory in social psychology and marketing,[51] its continuing popularity in consumer research no doubt results from the need to account for the post decisional dissatisfaction shown by many buyers of relatively expensive and infrequently purchased items, and for the fact that signs of dissonance tend to diminish as consumers use and/or otherwise familiarise themselves with the object of their purchase.[56]

This may be a special case of the phenomenon noted by Zajonc in which 'mere exposure' to an unfamiliar object is associated with an increase in liking for it: in one experiment, students confronted with an unknown individual who attended lectures 'enveloped in a big black bag' initially showed signs of hostility towards the object, followed by curiosity and 'friendship'.[57] The conclusion drawn by Zajonc from a review of experimental evidence is, on balance, 'in favour of the hypothesis that mere repeated exposure of an individual to a stimulus object enhances his attitude towards it.'[58] Presumably, the individual's initial reaction depends upon the negative reinforcement he has previously received as a result of interacting with novel objects; the absence of negative reinforcement in the experimental situation extinguishes avoidance behaviour and actions in which the individual is in close proximity to the unknown item (interpreted as 'friendship' in the example cited above) increase. Whatever explanation is accepted, however, the evidence on mere exposure and attitude change, like the phenomena which are the subject of the dissonance reduction hypothesis, reduce the importance of any pre-behavioural mental processes, pre-purchase problem solving and deliberative decision making. In doing this they suggest that the effects of behaviour upon attitudes or verbalisation need to be more consistently investigated.

A final observation on attitudinal–behavioural dynamics derives from the tendency of communications researchers to concentrate upon attitudinal change and merely to assume subsequent, corresponding behavioural modification. The Yale communications research programme, to which reference has been made, has been concerned with the effects of such factors as source credibility, and message organisation upon changes in recipients' attitudes or verbal behaviour. There is, of course, no reason to expect subsequent consistency between overt behaviour and the verbal responses to questionnaires from which attitude is assessed and attitudinal change inferred unless situational factors remain constant. Social psychologists in communications research have recently been criticised by Miller for their lack of concern about the prediction of behaviour:

> Out of the hundreds of persuasion studies conducted, only a handful have obtained a second behavioural measure to correlate with the attitude index; and even when such measures occasionally have been obtained, they have usually been nothing more than a second verbal report of anticipated future actions or ostensible after-the-fact behaviours. Thus, unless one assumes pervasive laziness or remarkable naivete, the inescapable conclusion seems to be that most persuasion researchers do not care about other behaviours, preferring instead to treat attitude as the focal point of enquiry.[59]

Consumer researchers also continue to evince preoccupation with the attitudinal dynamics which result from source credibility, fear appeals, and the like and to ignore or speculate about the nature of any consequent behavioural dynamics.[60] Behavioural choice dynamics, the prediction of which lies at the heart of commercial marketing research and which should, therefore, be a central concern of academic consumer research and theory, are still assumed to follow in some way from the modification of mental attitudes.

SITUATIONAL INFLUENCE

Like their cousins in general social psychology, consumer researchers before 1970 attributed much of the lack of demonstrated consistency between 'psychological' measures such as personality variables and attitudes and behavioural criteria such as overt action to situational influences but did little to investigate the effects of situational factors upon behaviour. During the last decade the direct examination of situational effects has become increasingly apparent among consumer researchers. A dominant theme in their work remains, however, the use of situational measures to improve correlations of intrapersonal events and overt behaviour. Bearden and Woodside report that the inclusion of situational measures significantly increased the prediction of behavioural intention from attitude data.[61] Their conclusion that their results, 'support the hypothesis that situations are influential in the formation of behavioural intentions and that a better understanding of choice behaviour is possible if more than attitudinal measures are used to explain behaviour'[62] represents what has become a commonplace observation in consumer research.

Such studies as this have advanced the recognition of the importance of situational factors for the prediction of behaviour but, insofar as they concentrate on the prediction of intentions, they ignore these factors and it is knowledge of these which is vital for the making of the accurate predictions required for effective marketing. The investigation of situations as direct inter-subjective ('objective') influences upon behaviour owes much to the work of Belk.[63] Among other contributions, Belk has proposed a definition and framework to guide the study of consumer purchasing situations which deserves consideration.

Defining Situations

Most investigations of consumer choice involve measurements of personal factors and/or product and their interactions. Belk draws attention to the situation in which choice occurs as a separate influence upon choice; situation is, 'something outside the basic tendencies and characteristics of the individual [such as traits and response dispositions], but beyond the characteristics of the stimulus object to be acted upon [e.g. product attributes].'[64] Both personal and object characteristics are assumed to be constant over a multiplicity of situations and unable, therefore, to be reckoned as situational components. Situation is defined accordingly as, 'all those factors particular to a time and place of observation which do not follow from a knowledge of personal (intra-individual) and stimulus (choice alternative) attributes and which have a demonstrable and systematic effect on current behaviour'.[65]

This definition portrays situations as intersubjectively specified ('objective') entities rather than as consumers' perceptions of their environments. Belk describes such situations in terms of five sets of features: *physical surroundings* such as decor, sound, weather, shelf height, lighting and temperature, *social surroundings* such as the presence of other people, their characteristics and roles, and interactions: *temporal perspective* which might be the time of day or season of year, purchase interval, constraints on time or the interval between shopping and consumption; *task definition* which includes reason for shopping and the role of the buyer. A person interested in buying a small appliance as a wedding present for a friend is in a different situation from that which obtains when he is shopping for a small appliance for his or her own use; and *antecedent states* such as acute moods, having cash on hand or illness.

Although Belk's influence upon the development of the study of purchasing in its situational context is widely acknowledged as a contribution to serious research it has not gone unchallenged. Lutz and Kakkar have argued against the 'objective' definition of situations and in favour of their subjective or 'psychological' specification, that is in terms of consumers' perceptions: accordingly a situation is 'an individual's internal responses to, or interpretations of, all factors particular to a time and place of observation which are not stable intra-individual characteristics or stable environmental characteristics, and which have a demonstrable and systematic effect on the individual's psychological processes and/or his overt behaviour'.[66] Although Belk has defended his approach on this count as well as against charges that it is too narrow or too broad,[67] the view of Kakkar and Lutz is clearly that objective measures of the situation are inadequate. They appear to accept that a purely subjective approach to situations is problematic in that the relationship between psychological responses and the external situation must be closely specified and that this has not been accomplished. But they show the eclecticism so characteristic of consumer researchers in stating that:

> The task for consumer behaviour researchers in this area . . . is that of combining the two approaches and investigating the mapping process which presumably precedes the impact of situational variables on behaviour. This mapping results in the translation of an objective situation into a psychological situation, the outcome of which flows into other psychological responses, decision processes, and behaviour.[68]

This statement, which closely resembles Hansen's approach,[69] is reminiscent of the argument that behaviour is mediated by internalised, mental events and processes, a paradigm which was shown in Chapter 3 to have serious drawbacks. Kakkar and Lutz make a more important criticism of Belk's approach, however, when they point out that his five descriptive dimensions of any situation involve extremely detailed accounts and enormous amounts of data which impede analysis.[70] This necessitates consideration of the research results which have been obtained with a variety of conceptual and analytical frameworks.

Belk's Findings

In order to clarify the nature of situational variables, Belk's early experiments will be described in some detail. 'Situation' as he defined it is narrower than the concept of a 'behavioural setting' such as a football game. Within the patterns and processes of so broad an event as a football match, Belk would recognise a multiplicity of situations: a particular goalmouth tackle in which a player has an opportunity to score might constitute a situation within the wide behavioural setting of the entire game.[71] An 'environment', according to Belk, is even broader than a setting in that it involves a permanent configuration of stable factors: geographical locations including football pitches, stadia, dressing rooms; intangibles such as rules of the game, previous judgements; social factors such as club officials, groundstaff, and so on. 'In this sense,' Belk argues, 'situations represent momentary encounters with those elements of the total environment which are available to the individual at a particular time.'[72] Even the five situational parameters mentioned by Belk present a wide perspective on the identification and measurement of situational variables which has been criticised by some writers.[73] In order to judge the viability of his approach, it is necessary to review his and subsequent empirical research.

In an exploratory study published in 1974, Belk investigated situational determinants of consumers' purchase and consumption patterns with respect to snack products and meat products.[74] Respondents indicated, in answers to questionnaires, their intentions to purchase particular products in specified situations. Ten snack foods (potato chips, popcorn, cookies, fresh fruit, sandwiches, pastries, ice cream, cheese, assorted nuts and crackers) were included in the survey together with a list of ten descriptions of hypothetical situations. These included: 'You are shopping for a snack that you or your family can eat while watching television in the evenings'; 'Snacks at your house have become a little dull lately and you are wondering what you might pick up that would be better'; 'You are thinking about what type of snack to buy to keep around the house this weekend.' The eleven meat products specified were: hot dogs, steak, chicken, hamburgers, hamburger dish/casserole, bologna, fish, pork chops, beef roast, luncheon meat and bacon. The hypothetical situations for these were: 'You are planning a party for a few friends and are wondering what to serve at dinner'; 'No one around the house has been very pleased with dinners lately and you are discussing what you might all try for dinner this weekend'; 'You are in a supermarket in front of the meat counter and are wondering what to buy in case friends or relatives drop by this weekend.'

Situational influence accounted for 15.8 per cent of the variance in snack product choice and 26.2 per cent of the variance in meat product choice. Belk concludes that:

> The most significant finding of this study concerns the amount of situational influence apparent in consumer food preferences. The fact that situational main effects and interactions provided nearly half of the explained variance in meat and snack preferences [there was a residual of 44.4 per cent unexplained variance in the case of snack products and 36.41 per cent in the case of meat products] strongly suggests that consumer research has much to gain by the explicit recognition of purchase and consumption situations.[75]

Table 4.1 *Illustrative studies of situational impact*

General situational characteristic*	Nature of consumer choice or behaviour	Associated situational factors	Authors
Physical surroundings			
including 'geographical and institutional location, decor, sounds, aromas, lighting, weather, and visible configurations of merchandise or other material surrounding the stimulus object'.	Search for information; composition of selected meal	Description of hypothetical restaurant in which 'meal' is ordered	Hansen
	Description of risk/uncertainty in purchase situation	Mail order vs. direct purchasing from retail outlet	Spence, Engel and Blackwell
Social surroundings			
'Other persons present, their characteristics, their apparent roles, and interpersonal interactions occurring . . .'		Presence of children	Wells and LoSciuto
		Presence of friends	Bell
		Presence of salesperson	Albaum
	Choice of brand of bread	Cohesiveness of social group	Stafford
	Choice of suit	Social compliance	Vankatesan

Table 4.1 *continued*

General situational characteristic*	Nature of consumer choice or behaviour	Associated situational factors	Authors
	Frequency of appliance sales	Bargaining similarity of buyer and salesman	Pennington
	Frequency of shopping trips, store choice, sources of information: purchases of groceries, domestic appliances, furniture	Social interaction, pre-purchase discussion, presence of significant others during shopping, location of residence	Foxall
Temporal perspective			
'. . . is a dimension of situations which may be specified in units ranging from time of day to season of the year. Time may also be measured relative to some past or future event . . . This allows conceptions such as time since last purchase, time since or until meals or payday, and time constraints imposed by prior or standing commitments.'	Value of supermarket purchases (obese vs. non-obese shoppers)	Time since last meal	Nisbett and Kanouse
	Total purchases of food products (obese vs. non-obese shoppers)	Time since last meal and provision of instore food sample	Steinberg and Yalch
	Discussion of innovative freeze dried coffee product	Previous discussion of food and coffee drinking	Belk
	Brand choice	Total product/brand portfolio	McAlister

Contin. overleaf

Table 4.1 continued

General situational characteristic*	Nature of consumer choice or behaviour	Associated situational factors	Authors
	Fast food restaurant selection; salience and description of product attributes; purchase frequency; description of convenience of restaurants	Lunch on weekday Snack during shopping trip Evening meal	Miller and Ginter
Task definition			
including 'an intent or requirement to select, shop for, or obtain information about a general or specific purchase.'	Simulated purchase of hairdryer as a gift	Description of roleplayer's wife	Hansen
	Sources and types of information for tableware	Purchase as gift vs. purchase for personal use	Grønhaug
	Fast food restaurant selection (see above)	Evening meal when rushed for time vs. evening meal when not rushed	Miller and Ginter
	Instore purchase propensity; scale of purchases by value	Credit card payment method in departmental store	Hirschman

Table 4.1 *continued*

General situational characteristic*	Nature of consumer choice or behaviour	Associated situational factors	Authors
Antecedent states and behaviour			
'These are momentary moods (such as acute anxiety, pleasantness, hospitality and excitation) or momentary conditions (such as cash on hand, fatigue and illness) rather than chronic individual traits. These states are further stipulated to be immediately antecedent to the current situation in order to distinguish states which the individual brings to the situation from states of the individual which result from the situation.' Immediately antecedent overt behaviour is also included.	Discussion of innovative freeze dried coffee product	Prior discussion of food and coffee drinks	Belk
	Choice of cigarette brands; consumption of beer	Conditioned boredom or stress	Sandell
	Total food purchases	Acceptance of food sample	Steinberg and Yalch

Sources overleaf

* Quotations are Belk's descriptions of general situational characteristics (see text).

Sources: Hansen, *Consumer Choice Behaviour*, pp. 472–5; H. E. Spense, J. R. Engel and R. D. Blackwell, 'Perceived Risk in Mail Order and Retail Store Buying', *Journal of Marketing Research*, vol. 7, no. 3 (1970) pp. 364–9; Wells and LoSciuto, 'Direct Observation of Purchasing Behaviour'; G. D. Bell, 'Self-Confidence and Persuasion in Car Buying', *Journal of Marketing Research*, vol. 4, no. 1 (1967) pp. 46–52; G. Albaum, 'Exploring Interaction in a Marketing Situation', *Journal of Marketing Research*, vol. 4, no. 2 (1967) pp. 168–72; J. E. Stafford, 'Effects of Group Influence on Consumer Brand Preferences', *Journal of Marketing Research*, vol. 3, no. 1 (1966) pp. 384–87; Vankatesan, 'Consumer Behaviour: Conformity and Independence', *Journal of Marketing Research*, vol. 3 (1966) pp. 384–7. A. L. Pennington, 'Customer–Salesman Bargaining Behaviour in Retail Transactions', *Journal of Marketing Research*, vol. 5, no. 3 (1965) pp. 255–62; Foxall, 'Social Factors in Consumer Choice', R. E. Nisbett and D. E. Kanouse, 'Obesity, Food Deprivation and Supermarket Shopping Behaviour', *Journal of Personality and Social Psychology*, vol. 12, no. 3 (1969) pp. 289–94; S. A. Steinberg and R. F. Yalch, 'When Eating Begets Buying: The Effects of Food Samples on Obese and Nonobese Shoppers', *Journal of Consumer Research*, vol. 4, no. 4 (1978) pp. 243–5; Belk, 'An Exploratory Assessment of Situational Effects'; L. McAlister, 'Choosing Multiple Items from a Product Class', *Journal of Consumer Research*, vol. 6, no. 3 (1979), pp. 213–74; K. E. Miller and J. L. Ginter, 'An Investigation of Situational Variation in Brand Choice Behaviour and Attitudes', *Journal of Marketing Research*, vol. 16, no. 1 (1979) pp. 111–23; Hansen, *Consumer Choice Behaviour*, pp. 122–6; K. Grønhaug, 'Buying Situation and Buyer's Information Behaviour', *European Marketing Research Review*, vol. 7 (1972) pp. 33–48; E. C. Hirschman, 'Differences in Consumer Purchase Behaviour by Credit Card Payment System', *Journal of Consumer Research*, vol. 6, no. 1 (1979) pp. 58–66; R. G. Sandell, 'Effects of Attitudinal and Situational Factors on Reported Choice Behaviour', *Journal of Marketing Research*, vol. 5 (1968) pp. 405–8.

These results offer encouragement but have been criticised on two counts. First, Lutz and Kakkar replicated Belk's study of snack products and found only six per cent of product choice variance to be explained by product-situation interaction.[76] They suggest that demand characteristics (i.e. interviewer or experiment induced bias) affected Belk's results. Belk subsequently presented results for beverages, fast foods, leisure activities and motion pictures which support his earlier conclusions and argued that the methodology employed by Lutz and Kakkar rendered their findings meaningless.[77] Secondly, as Belk himself points out, more direct observation and measurement of consumers' actual purchase behaviour are required in order that firm conclusions with respect to situational influences upon choice may be drawn. On the positive side, Belk's work has provided evidence that the inter-subjective definition of situational variables is capable of generating more managerially useful descriptions of contextual influences upon consumer choice than the approach which permits situations to be described solely and simply in terms of consumers' perceptions.[78]

There exists a considerable body of corroborative research findings, not all of them gained by research which was initially directed towards the clarification of situational influences upon consumer behaviour. Many studies of consumer behaviour have investigated some aspect or another of the situational dimension of choice and the small number of studies whose results are summarised in Table 4.1 are simply illustrative of the relevance of Belk's five general characteristics of situations. The accurate or at least consistent description by subjects of the moods and feelings in terms of which Belk describes antecedent states is not easily demonstrated. Experimental subjects in whom identical physiologically based states of arousal have been induced have variously described their affective and cognitive inferences.[79]

Although the results of these experiments have not gone unchallenged, the reliable description of emotional states remains problematic. Antecedent behaviour is included under the heading 'antecedent states' in this table in addition to Belk's description in order to emphasise the need to measure overt, inter-subjectively identifiable acts where possible as well as verbal descriptions of inner states.

Situations in Consumer Research

Students of buyer behaviour have drawn attention to the effect of situational contingencies upon choice and some have noted that situational factors may be so determinative as to preclude any pre-behavioural decision process. Baker presents purchase outcomes as a function of, *inter alia,* such *enabling conditions* as access to funds to spend or credit, *precipitating circumstances* such as unpredicted social events, and objective assessments of economic and technical performances.[80] And in his account of a model of industrial purchasing, Sheth points out that:

> The model described so far presumes that the choice of a supplier or brand is the outcome of a systematic decision-making process in the organisational setting. However, there is ample empirical evidence in the literature to suggest that at least some of the industrial buying decisions are determined by ad hoc situational factors and not by any systematic decision-making process.[81]

But, in spite of the growing recognition of situational determinants of consumer choice, there is no suggestion in the literature of

consumer behaviour that research should in general be directed towards the identification and measurement of situational or environmental influences rather than to delving further into consumers' internal psychological processes. The common expectation of consumer
researchers that any factors recently shown to be salient in the prediction of consumer choice can and should be assimilated by being
tacked on to existing analytical frameworks is apparent in reviewers'
evaluations of research into the situational context of choice. Kakkar
and Lutz survey both the intra-subjective approach to the study of
situational influences which is posited upon the assumption that situations should be described in terms of the phenomenology of the act-
ors involved, and the inter-subjective approach in which commonly
held descriptions are employed.[82] They do not choose between these
approaches or suggest that each may apply to the investigation of a
specific range of problems, but as has been noted, simply assert that
objective phenomena must be 'translated' into a psychological situation in order for behaviour to be affected. Despite the unequivocal
empirical evidence available with respect to the latent process view of
attitudes, the highly problematic attempts to investigate pre-behavioural decision processes, and to produce valid and consistent results, and the availability of an alternative framework of conception
and analysis, most consumer researchers do not appear to appreciate
the critical condition of their discipline. That situations shape and
maintain behaviour according to the contingencies of reinforcement
they contain is a proposition which hardly enters into the evaluation
of consumer choice. While situational and other environmental influences on choice are clearly being taken more and more seriously by
consumer researchers, none has as yet directly investigated the effects
of operant conditioning upon consumer behaviour. Nor has theoretical work in the area of situational influence upon consumer choice
appreciated that the importance of situations resides in the reinforcement contingencies they contain. Consistency of behavioural response is a function of situational consistency precisely because the
loci of behavioural control are to be found in the environment rather
than within the individual. A segment of consumer research is tending
in the direction of such reasoning, however; indeed, a small number of
experiments has been conducted to assess more accurately the effects
of incentives such as promotional offers or deals upon consumer
choice. In so far as this research has been concerned with the shaping
and maintenance of behaviour by extra-personal factors, it is of con-

siderable importance to the theme of this chapter and merits more detailed examination.

SELF-PERCEPTION

An interesting comment on attitudinal–behavioural consistency was made some two decades ago in a seminal paper by Campbell,[83] who emphasises the situational contexts in which verbal and overt behaviours occur and suggests that situations present constraints or 'hurdles' to behavioural expression. Expressing a positive attitude towards, say, a radically innovative product might well be to clear a hurdle which is relatively low compared with buying and publicly using the new item. A consumer who makes favourable verbal responses to the new product but who does not purchase it is not, therefore, showing inconsistency. Attitudinal–behavioural inconsistency would arise only if the consumer expressed a negative opinion of the product (thus failing to clear the initial, lower hurdle) but subsequently bought and consumed it openly. It would also presumably obtain should the verbal hurdle be higher than the overt behavioural hurdle and the customer surmounted the first but not the second – say by publicly endorsing an unpopular product but failing to buy it to use it personally. Such inconsistencies derive from situational dissimilarities.

Self-Perception Theory

Some consumer researchers have undertaken investigations of buyer behaviour which are based upon a logical foundation that is not inconsistent with Campbell's reasoning. Their work compares the attempt to alter or shape consumers' behaviour by means of persuasion based upon the cognitive information processing paradigm with attempts to modify behaviour directly through the manipulation of extra-personal loci of control including such promotional incentives as coupons, samples and money off offers. Two techniques, known respectively as 'foot-in-the-door' and 'door-in-the-face' have been employed on the premise that an individual who clears a very low behavioural hurdle (e.g. does a small favour for a friend) is likely subsequently to clear a rather higher hurdle (perhaps a bigger favour) and that an individual who refuses to clear a large hurdle (for example buy a month's supply of detergent rather than his usual week's supply) might nevertheless agree to compromise by buying two week's supply.

The theoretical justification for this approach stems, however, not from Campbell, but from Bem's self-perception theory, which was briefly mentioned in the last chapter as an alternative to cognitive dissonance theory as an explanation of the post behavioural attitude formation and change which have been so frequently observed by social psychologists. Bem put forward the view that attitudinal (verbal) behaviour represents self-description: the expression of favourable or unfavourable attitudes, likes and dislikes, comprises verbalised accounts of one's past behaviour.[84] The individual thus attributes preferences to himself by observing his own past behaviour and the statement 'I like football' is based upon the respondent's observation of his frequent attendance at football matches, purchase of football magazines, membership of a supporters' club, and so on. In other words, it is founded upon precisely the same order of observation made by other people when they attribute to that individual what they infer to be his attitude towards football and which results in the statement, 'He likes football'. Self-perceptions also underlie statements of behavioural intention which are thus confirmed by this theoretical model as relating to the past – to product usage in the case of consumer and consumption behaviour – and may, if circumstances allow, guide future actions.

One of the tenets of attribution theory is that individuals discriminate between those of their actions which appear to have been voluntary in the sense that they arise from and are guided by the individual's own attitudes and those which appear to have been constrained by situational factors such as the presence or opinions of others. A prediction derived from self-perception theory is that when individuals attribute the causation of their behaviour to their personal attitudes, beliefs or previous behaviour patterns and dispositions, they are more likely to continue to behave in a similar manner. A consumer who can find no external pressures to which to attribute his brand choice is thus predicted to repurchase the selected brand (if it otherwise functions adequately). When the consumer attributes his behaviour to external circumstances, such as lack of sufficient money or the availability of special offers or deals, he is more likely not to repurchase the chosen brand, at least once the offer is withdrawn or greater discretionary income becomes available.

Empirical Evidence

Three recently published reports of the testing of Bem's self-perception theory in marketing are of direct relevance to this chapter's assessment of trends in consumer research concerns. Scott's work begins with the comments that several experimental social psychological 'studies demonstrate that the provision of a reward or incentive for performing even an enjoyable or attitude consistent behaviour results in decreased intrinsic interest in subsequently engaging in that behaviour'[85] and that attempts to investigate this phenomenon in the marketing area has not so far produced conclusive evidence. Indeed, marketing presents certain peculiar problems in that incentives which have predictable impacts upon general social behaviour may be differently interpreted in commercial contexts where their widespread use may blunt their effectiveness.

In her empirical investigation, three discrete groups of consumers were each offered specific, small incentives in return for taking out a two-week trial subscription to a newspaper. The incentives were (i) a half price subscription, (ii) a free subscription and (iii) a free subscription plus a small additional gift. A fourth group was offered the paper on regular subscription during this initial phase of the research. At the end of the two-week trial, members of all four groups were asked to take out a regular subscription as were members of a fifth, control group of consumers who had not been previously contacted. Scott's experiment was designed to test the proposition derived from self-perception theory that those consumers who initially purchased a trial subscription at the full price would attribute their buying to their 'positive dispositions towards the product' and would be more likely to continue subscribing than those consumers who were in a position to attribute their previous behaviour to the incentive they had received. The latter group would be no more likely to subscribe than consumers contacted for the first time during the second phase of the research.

The results indicate that only the group whose members were offered half priced subscriptions during the first phase produced a significantly higher proportion (at the 5 per cent level of probability) than the control group whose initial contact with the newspapers' sales staff occurred after the trial period. Scott interprets these results as partially confirmatory of her hypotheses and argues that the incentives proffered might not have been salient to some respondents. She concludes that:

since people may expect to be given some incentive by commercial firms, the half price offer may have been just sufficient to produce compliance with the trial request but not sufficient to result in the discounting of internal motivations. Apparently, in commercial contexts small incentives are not perceived as plausible external causes and thus do not act as discounting cues.[86]

Small incentives (reinforcers) appear 'necessary to gain the greatest benefits from a behavioural influence strategy'.[87] In terms of a behaviourist interpretation, it appears that the consumers' reinforcement history with respect to the nature, frequency and size of reinforcers offered by marketers determines the effect of subsequent 'incentives'. Rothschild and Gaidis point out that a comprehensive behavioural learning strategy would have required the shaping of consumer behaviour over time rather than the provision of a single incentive.[88] Behavioural learning theory would, in fact, predict that operant behaviour would be quickly extinguished upon the removal of the reinforcer. They interpret these results by noting that, 'the incentive, and not the product, was the primary reward for purchase behaviour. When it was withdrawn, the behaviour was extinguished'.[89]

Dodson, Tybout and Sternthal report on the basis of an investigation of consumers' brand switching and repeat purchase behaviours, which is also based upon self-perception theory, that the provision of promotions encourages consumers to switch brands but that different types of promotion or deal have rather different effects: 'Media-distributed coupons induced substantial switching, cents-off deals somewhat less switching, and package coupons either decreased or did not affect brand switching.'[90] The withdrawal of promotions also had differential effects upon consumers' repeat buying. Both 'loyal' customers, those who purchase the brand in question before and after the media coupon promotion, and consumers who switched to that brand to take advantage of that promotion tended to switch to other brands when the deal was retracted. The withdrawal of money off offers was also associated with the abandonment of repeat purchasing by loyal and switching consumers. (This result was statistically significant at the 5 per cent level for margarine, but not for flour.) Those customers who regularly purchased brands of both products before a package distributed coupons promotion remained loyal after the withdrawal of that deal. The withdrawal of coupons distributed via the media undermined repeat buying to a lesser degree than the retraction of money off offers as package distributed coupons; and, finally, money off promotions undermined repeat buying more than did package distributed coupons.

The theoretical implications of these results are generally supportive of the self-perception approach. The amount of brand switching was in proportion to the size of incentive offered. More significantly, however, self-perception theory would predict that customers would not remain loyal to a brand with which large incentives requiring comparatively little effort on the part of the buyer (for example, media coupons or money off offers) were associated, once the promotion was withdrawn. Furthermore, the withdrawal of a smaller incentive which required greater effort of the buyer (for example, package coupons) would not, according to this theory, result in a significant reduction in loyalty. These hypotheses were supported by the results obtained by Dodson, Tybout and Sternthal who point out that, 'Support for the theory also obtains from the finding that retraction of media-distributed coupons resulted in less loyalty than retraction of either cents-off deals or package coupons.'[91]

Again Rothschild and Gaidis interpret the rather weak, albeit often statistically significant, relationships reported by these investigators of self-perception theory in terms of behavioural learning theory.[92] The inducement of brand switching attributed to large, easily obtained incentives simply indicates that those deals were highly reinforcing. The promotional record is more likely to be a stronger reinforcer than the product itself, however. The lack of attention to shaping consumer behaviour accounts, according to a behaviourist interpretation, for the extinction of brand buying behaviour upon the removal of the reinforcer.

In the third investigation, Tybout examined the effectiveness of foot-in-the-door, door-in-the-face and straightforward persuasion as methods of encouraging social security recipients to enrol in a health care plan.[93] Contrary to the author's expectation that the door-in-the-face technique (operationalised as a considerable request followed by a more moderate request) would result in greater behavioural change than either straight persuasion (an informative message) or the foot-in-the-door approach (a small request followed by a moderate appeal), none of these techniques emerged as significantly superior to the others. In addition, Tybout's use of message source credibility as an additional independent variable is consistent with the argument advanced by Dholakia that high levels of source credibility may act as discounting cues: although behavioural change may occur in situations of high source credibility, the individual's attribution of causal power to such an external influence militates against the continued performance of the induced response.[94]

Implications for Self-Perception Research

The handful of reported investigations of consumer choice which are tests of self-perception theory do not constitute full tests of behavioural learning theory in marketing. Some of the predictions of these theories are similar but tests of behaviourist theories in the sphere of consumer behaviour would require greater emphasis upon shaping and the manipulation of contingencies of reinforcement than is apparent in the work which has been briefly reviewed in this chapter. The import of these investigations in this discussion derives from their demonstration of the willingness of a few consumer researchers to consider influence strategies which do not rely directly upon the persuasion paradigm. Scott states that, 'persuasive strategies are predicated on the assumption that behaviour can be modified by influencing its cognitive precursors'[95] and notes briefly that this assumption is related to the search for knowledge about consumers' use of information and attitudinal–behavioural relationships. Behavioural influence strategies, conversely, 'focus on altering behaviour directly. These strategies are guided by the assumption that experience with a product or service constitutes an important basis for subsequent purchase action.'[96]

The implication of the investigation of behavioural rather than persuasive influence is that some consumer researchers are so dissatisfied with the prevailing paradigm that they are willing to look elsewhere for insights into the nature of consumer choice and its determinants. The particular interpretation of self-perception theory employed by these researchers allows considerable scope for considering consumers' cognitive interpretations of their behaviour as well as the behaviour itself: Scott speaks, for instance, of, 'the desirability of being attuned to the phenomenological meaning of behaviour.'[97] The work which has been discussed in this section has, moreover, failed to make full recognition of Bem's theoretical orientation. Bem identifies himself as a radical behaviourist.[98] His development of self-perception theory, as has been stated, was an attempt to provide an alternative explanation of the phenomena which are the basis of cognitive dissonance theory. This theory, Bem has written:

attempts to account for observed functional relations between stimuli and responses by postulating some hypothetical process within the organism, in this case, an inferred process of the arousal and reduction of dissonance . . . [D]issonance theory is further characterised by an emphasis on the individual's current phenomenology; the explanatory account in the theory itself is ahistorical.[99]

Self-perception theory, in stark contrast:

eschews any reference to hypothetical internal processes and seeks rather to account for observed functional relations between current stimuli and responses in terms of the individual's past training history. It remains our conviction that the appeal to hypothetical internal states of the organism for causal explanations of behaviour is often heuristically undesirable. Such diversion appears only to retard and deflect the thrust of the analysis that is ultimately required.[100]

Consumer researchers are unwilling to go to these lengths, to abandon the notion of internal, guiding states of mind, to reduce attitudes to the status of self-descriptions and agree with Bem that 'I like brown bread because I see myself eat it.'[101] But the use in consumer research of a theoretical approach which is not derived from the persuasion perspective implies that some marketing academics are seeking a way out of the critical state of research that is carried but within the cognitive information processing framework. The adoption of, even the movement towards, a behavioural learning paradigm has profound implications for consumer research in industry and for the pursuit of marketing management. These implications are the subject of the concluding chapter.

SUMMARY AND CONCLUSION

It has not been the intention of this chapter to provide, in rather typical textbook fashion, an uncritical review of the entire range of consumer behaviour and consumer research. Rather, the chapter has consisted of a discussion of trends in academic consumer research which are directly relevant to the two major paradigms which have provided conceptual and analytical frameworks for the study and pre-

diction of human behaviour. This discussion has been about the behaviour of consumer researchers as well as their investigations of consumer choice. In particular, it has focussed upon the inclinations of
consumer researchers to modify or extend the cognitive information
processing paradigm and to embrace behavioural learning theory as
an alternative.

In spite of the difficulty of confirming the information processing
models of consumer choice, this paradigm continues to dominate consumer research. Attitudinal-behavioural inconsistency has been demonstrated to occur unless the expression of attitudes is the immediate precursor of the relevant, overt behavioural act. There is
grave doubt surrounding the proposition that consumers usually engage in extensive, pre-behavioural problem solving. Yet the paradigm
from which this proposition and the expectation of a much more general level of demonstrable attitudinal-behavioural consistency derive
continues to generate large volumes of empirical investigation and
theoretical discussion.

This may well be evidential of a science in crisis as Kuhn describes
it:

> Recognising that something is fundamentally wrong with the
> theory upon which their work is based, scientists will attempt more
> fundamental articulations of theory than those which were admis-
> sible before . . . Simultaneously they will often begin more nearly
> random experimentation within the area of difficulty hoping to dis-
> cover some effect that will suggest a way to set the situation right.
> Only under circumstances like these, I suggest, is a fundamental
> innovation in scientific theory both invented and accepted.[102]

A full evaluation of the state of the art of consumer research would require many volumes. This chapter has only scratched the surface by
drawing attention to three spheres of research which are indicative of
trends in the overall discipline because of their centrality to the
paradigms under consideration. Perusal of the journals of marketing
research might well lead to the conclusion that the proliferation of
quasi-random empirical work and the generation of theories are indicative of a science in crisis. But there appears to be little conscious recognition of the shortcomings of the information processing approach
and no obvious predilection for a behaviourist framework to take its
place.

Yet the moves towards the serious investigation of the situational determinants of consumer choice and of behavioural influence strategies cannot be overlooked. Most researchers within these frameworks employ a theoretical model which contains a meld of environmental (extra-individual) and mentalistic (intra-personal) influences on consumer choice, but the former source of influence is now being emphasised in consumer research to a greater extent than before. There is, furthermore, evidence that some consumer researchers are willing to embrace behavioural learning theory if it proves relevant. In discussing the validity and implications of the results generated by his model of consumer choice, Sheth states that:

> We need to examine whether cognitively determined Affect and Behaviour or habitually determined Affect and Behaviour are more prevalent in consumer behaviour . . . The cognitively determined attitudes and behaviour will suggest the usefulness of persuasive communication as the strategy of change, and the behaviourally determined attitudes and behaviour will suggest the strategy of some form of behaviour modification.[103]

This suggests a willingness to be convinced of the value of behaviour modification though the cognitive psychological basis of much of Sheth's work is still apparent.

Even some behaviourist psychologists have shown a tendency to incorporate intrapersonal factors in their analyses. That consumer researchers retain these all too familiar variables while exploring more fully the external determinants of behaviour is perhaps inevitable. Taken with Kassarjian's suggestion that marketing scientists investigate an approach to the study of consumer choice which is more informed by behavioural learning theory, and the assessments of the feasibility of this course presented by Nord and Peter, and Rothschild and Gaidis, the developing interests of consumer researchers in behaviour itself rather than cognition alone, may suggest that a very slow paradigmatic transition is taking place. Paradigm shift, or at least the incorporation of a behaviourist approach within the repertoire of consumer researchers, must wait upon the execution of much more empirical research, the analysis of its results and the interpretation of its implications for both marketing study and practical management. Nevertheless, it is possible to draw conclusions from the analysis presented in these chapters and to develop immediate implications for the conduct of both academic and commercial consumer research and for marketing management.

Chapter 5

From Consumer Research to Marketing Management: Conclusions and Implications

INTRODUCTION

Previous chapters have been concerned with consumer choice in ways which are directly relevant to commercial marketing research and management as well as to the establishment and progress of a body of scientific knowledge. 'Consumer behaviour' is no longer a series of actions executed by buyers: it is an emergent discipline with implications for marketing research, business management, consumer education and protection, home economics and a host of other professions and fields of study. It is too early to draw fast conclusions for each and every implicated field but it is certainly appropriate to indicate broadly the import of the argument which has been pursued as a basis from which consequences for marketing thought and practice may be drawn and assessed.

The author's primary concern has been with the development of consumer behaviour as a discipline and as a resource upon which educationalists, researchers, managers and others might draw. Thus, the conclusions and implications discussed in this chapter initially concern the paradigm within which academic consumer researchers have conducted research and teaching. The subsequent discussion, the focus of which is consumer research, necessarily touches, however, upon both academic and commercial investigations of consumer choice, for each tends to rest upon the prevailing paradigm and any implications for that conceptual framework thus affect both theoreticians and practitioners. (Many consumer researchers have a foot in each camp, of course). The book cannot close at that point, however. Technologically based disciplines cannot advance unless they have strong links with practical concerns. It would be odd indeed if the paradigmatic questionings discussed in terms of pure and applied consumer research had no implications for marketing management.

An integral part of this chapter is devoted, therefore, to an exploratory account of the broad consequences of conceptual change for managerial action.

PARADIGMATIC IMPLICATIONS

DeFleur and Westie argue for the refinement of the concept of attitude by means of the elimination of an intervening or latent process variable and by the operational definition of attitude.[1] An essential step, 'would be to *link our definitions more firmly to the methods we employ in measurement*'.[2] They indicate the ramifications of this step quite clearly by pointing out that:

> We must start with the concept of attitude defined as specified probabilities of a syndrome of responses and then carefully specify three things: (1) the *exact* 'social object' which presumably provides the stimulation for these responses, (2) the *exact* nature and number of different classes or dimensions of responses [i.e., verbal or overt], and (3) the *exact* measuring or observational operations employed to obtain a quantitative statement of an individual's response probability for each class of responses.[3]

In large degree, their recommendations have been translated into action. The notion that 'true' attitudes are inner-state mechanisms, processes or hypothetical variables which mediate behaviour towards an object regardless of circumstance has been dealt a severe blow by the marshalling of empirical evidence to the contrary. The thorough going recognition of the prior importance of situational factors in the prediction of consumer choice is consistent with abandonment of the latent process conception and the adoption of a more probabilistic, behavioural conception of attitude.

The steps taken to ensure correspondence between verbal, attitudinal responses and overt behaviour, especially by the measurement of both behaviours on identical psychometric scales, have, moreover, linked definitions of attitude undeniably closely with the techniques of measurement that have been applied. But the adoption, conscious or unconscious, of a notion of attitude that is closely identifiable with De-Fleur and Westie's probability conception has more far reaching implications for marketing research and management than the redefinition and superior operationalisation of a central variable. It represents also a move in the direction of an alternative paradigm within which to conduct consumer research, to conceptualise the way in which marketing works and, therefore, to plan and evaluate marketing action.

To the extent that they have accepted a behaviourally based idea of attitude, both social psychologists and consumer researchers have moved from cognitive information processing as their fundamental anchorage point towards behaviourism, though both assuredly avoid extremes in the latter as much as in the former. The possibility of behaviourism being strengthened as a consumer research paradigm is obvious. Although as Chapter 4 demonstrated, it is too early to predict a general move in this direction, the weakening of the latent process conception of attitude and the calls by influential voices for a thorough examination of the place of behaviour theory in marketing make the following consideration of the accommodation of this alternative perspective highly relevant.

Eclecticism

There is no question of the behaviourist paradigm's suddenly replacing the prevailing framework of conception and analysis: as has been repeatedly pointed out, the social and managerial sciences rarely progress by means of revolution. Those authors who have advocated the use of the behavioural learning paradigm in marketing have also managed to argue that cognitive learning perspectives also have a place. Indeed, the eclecticism which characterises marketing's engagement with the behavioural sciences appears to be alive and flourishing. Behaviourist approaches cannot be ignored, however. The question that requires a response is: how can the behaviourist viewpoint be accommodated in marketing? The idea that behaviourist and cognitive psychologies can co-exist, each being employed in the study of a particular subset of human behaviour, is predictably anathema to those who adhere steadfastly to one or other of these philosophies. They do, after all, posit antithetical views of the causes and effects of human choice. But consumer research is a young science. Its practitioners are not seeking and evaluating paradigms in order that they may act as straightjackets. Rather, new perspectives are of use in the study of consumer behaviour insofar as they act like telescopes, microscopes or spotlights in rendering more accessible to the researcher the phenomena under investigation. When it becomes more appropriate to see the prevailing paradigm as a keyhole or a set of blinkers, change is inevitable as well as desirable.

It is possible, furthermore, to dichotomise consumer choice in such a manner as to accommodate the new framework whilst retaining the old. Most advocates of a behaviourally based paradigm have noted that its obvious place in consumer research may be the elucidation of low involvement behaviour. From his investigations of audience behaviour, Krugman concluded that, at least in the case of televisual advertising, consumer involvement is minimal, learning slow and unenduring, and behavioural change is necessary before attitudinal modification can occur.[4] He argues that, 'the learning of advertising [is] similar to the learning of the nonsensical or the unimportant. What is common to the learning of the nonsensical and the unimportant is lack of involvement'.[5] Perception or discrimination is not apparent until an opportunity to act arises, after which attitudes are changed. This is entirely consistent with the ideas that behavioural intentions are often inchoate until behaviour occurs and that attitudes are post behavioural self-descriptions. Krugman summarises the difference between low and high involvement behaviours by pointing out that:

> with low involvement, one might look for gradual shifts in perceptual structure, aided by repetition, activated by behavioural-choice situations, and *followed* at some time by attitude change. With high involvement one would look for the classic, more dramatic, and more familiar conflict of ideas at the level of conscious opinion and attitude that precedes changes in overt behaviour.[6]

This distinction finds support in both social psychology and consumer behaviour studies. Cialdini, Petty and Cacioppo summarise recent research by observing that:

> it now appears that attitude changes that occur through the central rather than the peripheral routes take place for different proximal reasons, through different psychological processes, and have difforrent long-term consequences. Accordingly, we suggest that they might best be viewed as distinct phenomena . . . When an individual's personal concerns are closely related to the attitude issue itself, change on the issue will likely come about primarily via the central rather than the peripheral route. For example, when issues

have been personally involving . . . persuasion has tended to be enduring.[7]

Comparatively few choices in the realm of consumer behaviour enter this category. Rather they are usually uninvolving with the consequence that changes have been 'transitory and situation specific.' Moreover, these authors note that 'when issues have been personally relevant . . . attitudes have been better predictors of behaviours than when the issues were relatively uninvolving'.[8]

Krugman's thesis has been applied to consumer behaviour in general by Robertson who reasons that it is probable that consumers are involved in a much smaller amount of pre-purchase information search than has usually been assumed.[9] Furthermore, trial is the most important means of brand evaluation, pre-trial learning being minimal. Furthermore, the processes of consumer choice postulated by theories of consumer behaviour lack feasibility because beliefs are weakly held and transient. Any hierarchy of effects that actually occurs is simple and contracted for consumer purchase choices. Speaking of 'commitment' rather than 'involvement', he concludes that:

> In high-commitment situations, the model of an active audience critically evaluating messages and countermessages and proceeding to purchase in a hierarchical learning response pattern is quite reasonable. In low-commitment situations, the model of a fairly passive consumer who does not seek nor critically evaluate most messages and who may act in a simple awareness – trial response pattern seems more reasonable. A large share of consumption is trivial, unimportant, and non-ego involving, such that beliefs and preferences are not strongly held and there is a lack of commitment to the existing purchase modality.[10]

The possibility that a behavioural learning paradigm is required in order to understand and predict low involvement consumer choice while cognitive psychology is better able to explain high involvement choice is intriguing but must remain a hypothesis in the absence of clear-cut evidence. Certainly the possibility of a useful 'fit' is strong. In the words of Cialdini, Petty and Cacioppo:

> The central route [which occurs when an individual can think and is motivated about an issue] emphasises a thoughtful consider-

ation of the attitude issue whereas the peripheral route [which occurs when ability to think and/or motivation is low] emphasises aspects of the persuasion situation that are clearly tangential to the issue under consideration (e.g. the rewards available for advocating a certain view; the attractiveness of the message's source, etc.[11]

This certainly suggests a cognitive/behavioural dichotomy upon which further research might advantageously focus. Furthermore, consumer researchers have already found a place for the distinction: in the fourth edition of *Consumer Behaviour*, Engel and Blackwell advance two models of consumer choice, one for high involvement behaviour, the other for low involvement behaviour.[12] The relevance of a behavioural learning model might well be established by reference to well established typologies in consumer research such as those based upon inner and other direction, social class variations, cultural differences and so on. Similarly there may be segments of consumers whose attitudes (verbal reports) provide much more accurate forecasts of behaviour than others; research would establish the extent to which such customers were definable.

Existence and Explanation

The selection of a research paradigm rests not simply upon a view of the nature of the phenomenal universe but upon deciding to which aspects of reality study should be directed. Cognitive psychology does not ignore behaviour any more than most behaviourists deny the reality of thinking or the importance of information. It is the invariable depiction of consumer choice in terms of complex, pre-behavioural, cognitive information processing which is an exaggeration, just as its depiction solely in terms derived from behaviourism is an exaggeration. Kuhn's idea of a mature science is one in which periodic surges in progress occur as a result of revolutionary paradigmatic supersession. Perhaps mature *social* sciences are necessarily multi-paradigmatic, their maturity stemming from the judicious application of relevant paradigms according to the nature of the problem under investigation.

This book has not only shown that the cognitive information processing paradigm has greater shortcomings than are usually recognised; it has also noted the possibility of an alternative, at least with respect to the study of consumers' attitudes. But the behavioural learning paradigm provides only very restricted explanations. In the case of attitude, if this concept is defined in terms of response consistency, it is clear that its use as an 'explanation' of behaviour is tautological. Such a descriptive rather than explicatory approach is not new to marketing. It has been encountered in the work of Ehrenberg[13] and in the depiction of consumer choice as a probabilistic or stochastic process.[14] But it nevertheless represents a large step from the 'explanation' of choice in terms of internal, psychological process which are so familiar in the literature of consumer behaviour and it is important that those who work within this paradigm are aware of the nature of the 'explanations' it offers.

There are, of course, many students of human behaviour for whom this line of explanation is no more tautological than the ascription of mental causation to overt action. Skinner, for instance, questions the beliefs that 'a mental event can cause or be caused by a physical one' and that the key to the prediction of behaviour lies in the discovery of a quite different class of event known as a state of mind.[15] The problem with mentalistic explanations, or explanations which attempt to combine mental and environmental causation is, he holds, that they posit 'that three stage sequence in which the physical environment acts upon the organism to generate mental or psychic activities, some of which ultimately find expression in physical action. The puzzling question of how a physical event causes a mental event, which in turn causes a physical event, remains to be answered or dismissed as unanswerable.'[16]

Several far reaching issues derive from the discussion of attitudes, intentions and behaviour which has occupied much of this book. How far should consumers' responses to attitude measuring instruments be regarded as expressions of 'true', underlying attitudes which consistently mediate verbal and overt behaviours? How far should questionnaire responses be viewed as a class of behaviours controlled by one set of contingencies of reinforcement, while overt actions belong to another class of behaviours which are governed by separate reinforcers? Under what circumstances, then, can attitudinal-behavioural consistency be predicted? These are key questions for marketing education, research and practice.

Is it necessary to posit intervening processes in order to explain behaviour? Or should marketers assume that the causes of behaviour are external to the individual? This may be less an issue about what actually exists or about what covert events occur within individuals and more an issue that relates to our selection of predictors of behaviour which are relevant to the marketing task. As such it is a paradigmatic issue whose theoretical and practical consequences for marketing are immense. Its resolution depends upon research and the interpretation of research.

IMPLICATIONS FOR CONSUMER RESEARCH

Attitudes and Behaviour Revisited

It is evident, irrespective of any paradigmatic implications, that verbal or 'attitudinal' behaviour is *likely* to be predictive of overt behaviour only to the extent that it involves identical contingencies of reinforcement which may be subsumed by similar situational factors. Research in other areas of social science has demonstrated that where signing a petition while standing on one's own doorstep is the measured overt behaviour in question, the appropriate situation for the prior recording of verbal intentions is that same doorstep.[17] Similarly, when volunteering to be subjects in psychological experiments is the overt behaviour, the highest behavioural consistency is apparent when the verbal intention to do so is obtained in the same physical setting.[18] The achievement of a corresponding degree of consistency in the context of consumer choice would require the recording of consumers' intentions in the same physical, geographical, social and economic situations in which buying takes place. Closely related to this is the need to measure attitudes and behaviour at the same level of specificity or, more accurately, in ways that fulfil the requirements of correspondence in terms of the four elements (action, target, context and time) distinguished by Ajzen and Fishbein.[19]

Such achievement has, more often than not, been absent from research on brand attitudes, though an increasing emphasis on the measurement of attitude-towards-the-act rather than attitude-towards-the-object clearly increases situational correspondence to some degree. A practical question for consumer researchers concerns the extent to which the measurement of attitude-towards-the-act can substitute for the recording of behavioural intentions in the buying situation. Mostyn notes, moreover, the common practice of measuring attitudes by means of a multi-point Likert-type scale while behaviour is measured in terms of a rough continuum comprising the response categories 'buy regularly', 'buy once in a while' and 'never buy'.[20] To the extent that consumer researchers in academic as well as commercial investigations continue to devise separate scales for the measurement of verbal and overt behaviours, their work is unlikely to predict consumer brand choice.

The elapse of time between the expression of a purchase intention and the next opportunity to purchase is also of critical significance. The highest correlations of BI:B, employing the Fishbein intentions model, have been obtained when behaviour followed immediately upon the recording of intentions. The implication is that the accurate prediction of behavioural choice is possible over only relatively short time spans. This is not a criticism of the Fishbein model; indeed its author has been quite explicit that in his approach *BI* is the immediate antecedent of *B*, a factor which consumer researchers appear to have overlooked. The number of occasions when the prediction of behaviour from its immediately antecedent intentions is useful or possible in consumer research is severely limited so say the least. Perhaps more frequent reinvestigation of behavioural intentions, appraisal of *current* purchase behaviour and control of marketing action, plus the employment of identical psychometric scales in the measurement of intentions and behaviour would increase the validity of predictions. But the conclusion must surely be that those aspects of marketing research which rely upon attitudinal-intentional-behavioural correspondence and the prediction of overt buying behaviour from prior verbal behaviours requires comprehensive reappraisal.

Another issue is the need to ensure, in consumer research and particularly in applied investigations, that behaviour itself is the dependent variable. Because of the nature of the Fishbein intentions model – particularly its assumption that any behaviour to be predicted is that behaviour which immediately follows the expression of a corresponding intention – it matters little in validational work that BI is often the dependent variable. In the case of consumer research the ability of a research instrument to predict behaviour in a given situational context is of paramount importance. Fishbein and Ajzen present interesting evidence of the internal validity of their model to measure intentions in the realm of consumer choice but this is of little value in the prediction of consumer behaviour some weeks, months or years hence. New product development relies upon the use of consumers' expressions of likes and dislikes of no more than product concepts, prototypes or market test experiences. Vital decisions are made at several stages of the innovative process on the basis of potential customers' verbal reports of their hypothetical future behaviour. Even the most sophisticated research tools can act only upon the data supplied: when those data refer to consumers' verbal behaviour which have little or no predictive validity, the high level of failure in new consumer product markets is more readily explicable.

The Fishbein Intentions Model

The application of Fishbein and Ajzen's thinking to consumer research is undeniably an important step forward. As they have noted, the simple recording and measurement of customers' evaluative beliefs with respect to product or brand attributes is not a sufficient basis upon which to predict choice. Beliefs about and evaluations of a given attribute may not be salient in the specific purchase situation presented to the customer. Furthermore, attitudes towards a brand, even though accurately measured, need not predict behaviour with the brand in specified circumstances, 'The reasons for buying or not buying a given product are not the same as the reasons for liking or not liking it. Many parents who detest breakfast cereals buy them regularly.'[21] Rather, 'the purchase of a given product is ultimately determined by beliefs concerning the positive and negative consequences of the purchase and the normative prescriptions of important referents'.[22] These authors' demonstration of the crucial importance of measuring attitudes and behaviour in corresponding terms is sufficient to identify the major weaknesses in this department of consumer research. That this is being rectified is indicative of considerable progress.[23]

Yet there remain deep problems in the operational use of the Fishbein intentions model in the prediction of consumer choice in ways which are managerially useful. Allusion has been made to the difficulty of elapsed time between intentions and behaviour. The model simply is not concerned with the prediction of future events upon the basis of today's measurements of intention. Another difficulty arises from the attempt to insure that attitudes and behaviour are measured at a corresponding level of specificity. Schuman and Johnson note that the measuring of specificity is ambiguous, varying from one investigation to another, 'We are given a general direction in which to proceed, but the destination remains theoretically imprecise.'[24] The search for correspondence may become self defeating if specification becomes too detailed. Commenting upon LaPiere's study, Fishbein and Ajzen argue that to ask whether a restaurateur or hotelier would accept a Chinese couple is to employ too incomplete and ambiguous an attitude object.[25] They suggest that different results would have been obtained had the attitude object been 'a young, well-spoken, pleasant, self-confident, well-to-do Chinese couple accompanied by a mature, well-dressed, well-spoken . . . educated European gentleman'. Of course, this renders attitude measurement too difficult and is likely to generate results which lack generality.[26]

Ehrenberg and Goodhardt argue that the marketing equivalent of the response to a single social situation with which the intentions model is concerned is the consumer's behavioural response to a product class.[27] If, as these authors argue, brands within a product class are usually perceived by users and non-users of the product as possessing identical attributes, the model does no more than record that a brand is seen as belonging to a general class of interchangeable brands. This being so, it is unlikely to permit the required level of specificity to be reached in consumer research. Even if correspondence in terms of target, action, context and time is achievable in consumer research, the results would relate to such specific behaviours as to be of little value say in the segmentation of markets and the creation of differentiated marketing programmes. The perceived consequences of brand A rather than brand B (target), of buying rather than consuming or leasing it (action), for personal use rather than as a gift (context) and today rather than in a month (time) add up to a very specific act that is of limited interest to marketing decision makers.

Situational Buying Behaviour

Similar difficulties apply to the direct study of the situational determinants of consumer choice. Once more, highly specific behaviours are involved. The implication is that consumer research might provide more accurate forecasts of choice if more general features of situations can be isolated. Behavioural learning theory deserves attention in this regard and consumer research might be profitably directed towards such issues as the most appropriate forms of shaping and modelling effects and the replication of the research programmes whose results support behaviour based approaches in the non-laboratory, voluntaristic contexts offered in consumer purchasing situations. The identification of appropriate schedules of reinforcement for the enhancement of shaping and modelling effects, perhaps along the lines suggested by Rothschild and Gaidis (see Chapter 2) appears to hold considerable promise for research based marketing management. Such a programme of resarch would not require completely new tools of investigation: consumers' verbal reports may, for instance, provide useful information about their reinforcement histories as well as the contingencies of reinforcement governing the provision of such reports. Like so much in consumer research, their validity can only be determined by painstaking empirical examination and analysis.

By moving towards the investigation of situational determinants of choice, consumer research is following the lead of a significant number of social psychologists who have concluded that a central concern of the application of their discipline is 'the need to understand the processes involved in the transactions between people and their surroundings; what may be called a theory of person-environment interaction.'[28] The research tools, methods of analysis and canons of professional judgement required for the progress of the study of consumer choice in its environmental context are, therefore, likely to be increasingly available. Such tools, methods and criteria should permit consumer researchers to improve substantially upon previous consumer research in which situations have tended to be ignored or inadequately defined and in which the contingencies of reinforcement are seldom the same in both verbalising situations and buying situations. The possibility held out by an approach to consumer research which is more behaviourally based is that investigators will find it preferable to discover what consumers actually do in specified buying and consumption situations and to calculate the probabilities of particular choices recurring. This issue and the extent to which verbal and overt behaviour can be measured in such a manner as to allow the latter to be predicted from the former are, at present, intriguing questions. Deciding the place of any formal representations of cognitive processes in the shaping and maintenance of behaviour by experience must also wait upon the execution of innovative research.

MANAGERIAL IMPLICATIONS

The definition of measurement in terms of behavioural consistency rather than mental states and processes has important implications for marketing management. Such definition involves a radically different understanding of consumer choice from that which currently prevails. To the extent that consumer behaviour is reinforced by its consequences and derives its consistency/and thus its predictability/from the contingencies of reward which reside in the situations in which buying and consumption occur, managerial action should address itself to considering the environmental factors which determine consumer choice and repeat buying. To the extent, moreover, that reference to internal, latent processes becomes redundant in the explanation and prediction of consumer choice, marketing management ought to de-emphasise consumers' information processing. The key phrase is 'to the extent that' since the research upon which fine discriminations between these approaches to managerial action depend has yet to be undertaken. Indication of the precise consequences for management of a behaviour based approach to consumer choice must, therefore, wait. The following comments are, then, necessarily general.

It would be a relatively simple task merely to recast familiar descriptions of marketing practices in less well known, behaviourist jargon. 'Selective perception' would become 'a discriminative response'; the use of reference group figures in advertisements would become 'modelling'; and the use of haunting tunes and bright colours in promotional materials would be described in terms of classical (respondent) conditioning. There is no harm in this, and the research which is now proceding within such a framework may suggest novel managerial outcomes.[29] The analysis presented earlier in this book, especially in Chapter 3, and the conclusions which have been drawn from it demand answers to more fundamental questions, however. First, how far are the conclusions which have been reached applicable beyond the purchase of repeatedly purchased consumer goods which have thus far been the primary focus of the discussion? And, secondly, what are the implications for managerial action of the comprehension of consumer choice as the result of a process which is akin to Ehrenberg and Goodhardt's 'weak' theory of marketing rather than as the outcome of a 'strong' hierarchy of effects process?

The Scope of the Argument

It is generally accepted that the purchase of fast moving consumer goods involves rather different pre- and post decisional processes

from those involved in buying consumer durables or industrial products. Risk, frequency and magnitude of purchase, social and
economic influences and the complexity of decision making are all
factors commonly brought up to account for the differences. The
behaviourist argument might be more easily accepted in the case of
regularly purchased consumer products which represent low involvement and relatively unimportant choices. It is, perhaps, fairly clear
that, in such cases, choice is determined largely by the consequences
of previous behavioural choices which have occurred in similar situations. Behavioural learning and the habitual behaviour it leads to
constitute an obvious strategy where risk can be managed through the
replicated selection of a single brand or the confinement of choice to a
few similar brands within a homogeneous product class.

The purchase of consumer durables and industrial goods and ser-
vices cannot usually be managed in so straightforward a manner.
Schedules of reinforcement in these situations are often such that the
learning of brand related responses is slower and more haphazard
than where fast moving goods are concerned. Nevertheless, the effects
of buyers' reinforcement histories is likely to be considerable simply
because they involve major purchases. The greater the extent of
economic cost/benefit and net performance appraisal which such relatively complex choices incur, the more probable it is that purchase
outcomes are determined by the consequences of past actions[30] Given
this there appears to be no evident constraint upon the range of
applicability of behavioural learning theory in marketing on *a priori*
grounds. The similarity of these various forms of consumer behaviour
is an empirical issue to which behavioural learning theory based investigation might well be addressed.

Consumer Trial and Repeat Buying

Just as there appears to be no reason to confine a behavioural learning
approach to the purchase and consumption of any particular type of
product, so it need not be limited to a specific stage in the buying process such as post trial repeat purchasing. The impression that it might
be thus circumscribed could arise from the support accorded by the
foregoing analysis of attitudinal–behavioural relationships to the
'weak' theory of advertising: if attitudes are formed at all with respect
to brand purchasing and consumption, their formation is predicted to
occur *after* purchase and trial. Indeed, according to the probability

conception, attitudes are determined by and, indeed, comprise patterns of brand loyalty for they are defined as the consistency of behaviour. In line with this, it might be argued that a brand trial, which involves discontinuous innovations or continuous use of a brand which has not been previously purchased, entails relatively high involvement consumer behaviour, contingent upon persuasive advertising and internal information processing. If the logic of such an argument were accepted, behavioural learning theories would be rendered superfluous at the pre-trial stage.

The behavioural learning theorist cannot argue with the proposition that advertising and promotional techniques encourage brand awareness and trial: indeed there are circumstances in which it is difficult to envisage a trial being stimulated by other than marketer dominated means. The more discontinuous or radical a new product, the more probable it is that the buying process is initiated by means of formal marketing communications. The diffusion of new products depends vitally upon the behaviour of consumer innovators whose sole source of information is marketer dominated since, at this stage of the diffusion of innovation, networks of informal communication can hardly have developed. A behaviour based approach offers, however, an explanation of the effects of advertising and promotions on brand trial which is distinct from the current view that marketing communications are effectual at this stage by virtue of their ability to create and strengthen mental attitudes which, in turn, motivate and shape behaviour. Rather, behaviourists would point out that consumers' observation of significant reference groups or *models* in advertisements, especially where such models are depicted using and benefitting from the brand in question, leads to vicarious learning on the part of the audience which is manifested in the acquisition of new purchase and consumption responses or in the inhibition or disinhibition of responses already acquired.[31] The traditional concerns of the school which portrays persuasive messages as strong influences on behaviour may be interpreted within a behaviour based framework as relating to previous reinforcement patterns and generalisation. A message source which has elicited behaviour which has had positively reinforcing consequences is likely to be believed when its subsequent messages refer to untried brands; or, more generally, reliance upon models whose recommendations have proved trustworthy in broadly similar buying contexts leads to the acceptance of other recommendations which have the same origin because similar contingencies of reinforcement seem likely to reoccur. Consumers will discriminate in favour of those message sources which have previously resulted in rewarding consequences.

Influencing Consumer Choice

While trial may occur as a result of vicarious learning, generalisation and discrimination repeat purchasing is probable only if the direct consequences of trial with the brand are positively reinforcing. Far more managerial attention should be given to the use of product features or attributes which primarily reinforce brand choice and to marketing communications, notably promotional deals, which act as secondary reinforcers. Current preoccupation with complex quantitative research tools such as conjoint analysis which attempts to measure consumers' reactions to different combinations of the attributes of a known product class[32] is of limited value unless the attribute combinations permit or lead to behavioural discrimination among brands rather than just the ability to make verbal or intellectual distinctions.

Shaping, which refers to the provision of a series of rewards for behaviours which progressively approximate the required response, may be accomplished by coupon offers, sampling and other related promotional reinforcers. As shown in the previous chapter, such techniques are at present inadequately employed in marketing. The provision of almost any promotional incentive is expected to go some way towards producing whatever behavioural response the marketer feels desirable; promotional campaigns are frequently planned and executed simply in order to counter competitors' campaigns with scant attention being paid to their net effect on consumer choice. The result is a style of management dominated by product considerations or short term sales enhancement rather than a genuine marketing orientation.

As a result, the benefits of promotional shaping are lost. This is generally a result of emphasis being placed upon the incentive itself which is at best only a secondary reinforcer rather than upon the product and its attributes, whose use provides consequences which reinforce subsequent discrimination either for or against a given brand. The use by marketers of smaller incentives and their concentration upon the reinforcing capacity of the brand itself are more likely to ensure that the withdrawal of promotional deals is not followed by the extinction of brand choice behaviour. The benefits of marketing communications based upon promotions are also frequently lost as a result of an emphasis upon once-for-all incentives which are unable to facilitate the learning of behavioural responses. Once again, the problem derives from a lack of planned shaping of consumer choice. The differential effects upon successive behavioural approximations to the required choice of various promotional methods can also be expected to form the basis of valuable consumer research and managerial action. As the work of Dodson, Tybout and Sternthal[33] which was reviewed in Chapter 4 suggests, direct financial offers may be superior to coupons in provoking brand trial while in/on-the-pack coupons may be more effective for the maintenance of brand choice than either financial deals or media distributed coupons. This pattern not only has the support of empirical research it is congruent with behavioural theory: as both financial rewards and media coupons involve non-product, secondary reinforcement, the extinction of brand choice responses on the withdrawal of the deal is entirely predictable. Finally, behavioural learning theory offers an explanation for the effectiveness of the defensive, non-persuasive use of advertising for most well established consumer brands which was noted by Ehrenberg and Goodhardt: the advertisement may itself constitute a reward for brand choice, especially if it includes the endorsement of a prestigious model. Although larger volumes of research are needed to discover the precise relevance of behaviourism to marketing, it is clear that the overall strategy implied by behavioural learning theory requires a quite different treatment of the concepts of 'attitude' and of attitudinal–behavioural relationships from that which is current. There is no question here of employing 'strong', 'persuasive' communications with the intention of altering latent processes and thus behaviour. Any 'hierarchy of effects' refers to the progressive shaping of behaviour through the planned provision of positively reinforcing consequences for brand related responses. If the concept of 'attitude' is required, it refers to the consistency of consumer response in various situational contexts and their attendant reinforcement contingencies.

FINAL SUMMARY AND CONCLUSION

A behaviourist interpretation of marketing phenomena is certainly feasible. There are major cracks in the prevailing, mentalist paradigm deriving notably from the inability of consumer researchers to demonstrate attitudinal-behavioural consistency irrespective of situational interventions. There is, moreover, evidence that the effects of situational variables on consumer choice is greater than has been generally appreciated. Cognitive approaches to the study of consumer behaviour are now faced with an alternative, competing paradigm. Kuhn's depiction of progress in natural and physical science in terms of paradigmatic supersession is unlikely to apply to the social sciences and this book has avoided the suggestion that cognitive psychology is about to give way to behaviourism in the context of marketing. But, just as the continual jostling of competing analytical and conceptual frameworks tends to be the norm in social sciences such as economics and sociology, so a more lively theoretical debate is now possible in marketing. The greater the emphasis placed upon probability concepts of attitude as a result of increasing recognition of the situational and environmental determinants of behaviour, and the greater the appreciation of the inadequacies of the latent process conception in the prediction of consumer choice, the more will behavioural learning theories become important for the investigation of consumer choice and for customer oriented marketing management.

Further Reading

CHAPTER 1

Most readers will find that a general introduction to the study of consumer behaviour is useful. Any of the following can be recommended in this respect as a concise, introductory account:

G. R. Foxall, *Consumer Behaviour: A Practical Guide* (London: Croom Helm; and New York: John Wiley, 1980).

T. S. Robertson, *Consumer Behaviour* (London: Scott, Foresman, 1970).

M. Tuck, *How Do We Choose? A Study in Consumer Behaviour* (London: Methuen, 1976).

CHAPTER 2

On the concept of paradigm and scientific progress:

T. S. Kuhn, *The Structure of Scientific Revolutions* (Chicago: Chicago University Press, 1970).

On psychological paradigms:

P. H. Lindsay and D. A. Norman, *Human Information Processing*, 2nd edn (New York: Academic Press, 1978).

R. D. Nye, *What is B. F. Skinner Really Saying?* (Englewood Cliffs: Prentice-Hall, 1979).

B. F. Skinner, *About Behaviourism* (London: Cape, 1974).

B. F. Skinner, *Beyond Freedom and Dignity* (Harmondsworth: Penguin, 1973).

For an interpretation of behaviourism which retains some aspects of human freedom, see:

F. Carpenter, *The Skinner Primer* (New York: Free Press, 1974).

CHAPTER 3

The following paper has much of value for students of attitudes and behaviour in marketing:

M. L. DeFleur and F. R. Westie, 'Attitude as a Scientific Concept', *Social Forces,* vol. 42, no. 1 (1963) pp. 17–31.

On the Fishbein intentions model and its applications, see:

I. Ajzen and M. Fishbein, *Understanding Attitudes and Predicting Social Behaviour* (Englewood Cliffs: Prentice-Hall, 1980).

and, at a deeper level:

M. Fishbein and I. Ajzen, *Belief, Attitude, Intention and Behaviour* (Reading, Mass.: Addison-Wesley, 1975).

CHAPTER 4

At this stage a general idea of the current status of consumer behaviour study may be useful. The following remains the most comprehensive guide:

J. F. Engel and R. D. Blackwell, *Consumer Behaviour,* 4th edn (Hinsdale, Illinois: Dryden, 1982).

It is also instructive to compare its content and structure with the third edition (Engel, Blackwell and Kollat, 1978). Note particularly the latest edition's bifurcation of consumer behaviour into 'high involvement' and 'low involvement' actions and the relegation of comprehensive, information processing models of consumer choice to an Appendix.

CHAPTER 5

The academic and professional journals are the best guide to the future of consumer research and marketing management. See especially in connection with consumer choice:

Journal of Consumer Research,
Journal of Marketing Research, and
European Research;

and, in connection with managerial response:

Journal of Marketing, and
European Journal of Marketing.

See also the reviews of consumer psychology which now appear regularly in the *Annual Review of Psychology,* e.g. H. H. Kassarjian's 'Consumer Psychology' in the 1982 issue, pp. 619–50, which addresses, *inter alia,* the issue of low commitment behaviour.

Notes and References

CHAPTER 1

1. J. Jacoby, 'Consumer Research: A State of the Art Review', *Journal of Marketing*, vol. 42, no. 2 (1978) pp. 87–96.
2. N. Brunsson, 'The Irrationality of Action and Action Rationality: Decisions, Ideologies and Organisational Actions', *Journal of Management Studies*, vol. 19, no. 1 (1982) p. 29.
3. B. Mostyn, *The Attitude–Behaviour Relationship* (Bradford: MCB Publications, 1978) p. 83.

CHAPTER 2

1. J. M. Keynes, *The General Theory of Employment, Interest and Money* (London: Macmillan, 1936) p. 383.
2. E. M. Woolley, 'Finding the Point of Contact', in *Advertising*, vol. VI of the Library of Business Practice (New York: A. W. Shaw, 1914) pp. 25–6.
3. C. D. Murphy, 'What Makes Men Buy', in *Advertising* (New York: A. W. Shaw, 1914) p. 9.
4. F. Hansen, 'Psychological Theories of Consumer Choice', *Journal of Consumer Research*, vol. 3, no. 3 (1976) p. 117.
5. Ibid.
6. J.-P. Sartre, *Being and Nothingness*, trans. H. E. Barnes (New York: Washington Square Press, 1973).
7. B. F. Skinner, *About Behaviourism* (London: Cape, 1974) p. 113.
8. T. S. Kuhn, *The Structure of Scientific Revolutions* (Chicago: Chicago University Press, 1970).
9. E. E. Jones and H. B. Gerard, *Foundations of Social Psychology* (New York: Wiley, 1967) p. 46.
10. Kuhn, *The Structure of Scientific Revolutions*, p. 230.
11. H. Thelen and J. Withal, 'Three Frames of Reference', *Human Relations* (April 1949).
12. For example, I. M. Kirzner, *Entrepreneurship and Competition* (Chicago: Chicago University Press, 1973); S. C. Littlechild, *The Fallacy of the Mixed Economy* (London: Institute of Economic Affairs, 1978).
13. For example J. H. Goldthorpe, 'A Revolution in Sociology?', *Sociology*,

vol. 7, no. 3 (1973) pp. 449–62; H. Garfinkel, *Studies in Ethnomethodology* (Englewood Cliffs: Prentice-Hall, 1967).

14. J. B. Watson, *Behaviour* (New York: Holt, 1914); *Behaviourism* (New York: People's Institute Publishing Co., 1924).

15. R. L. Solso (ed.), *Contemporary Issues in Cognitive Psychology: The Loyola Symposium* (Washington, D.C.: V. H. Winston and Sons, 1973); see especially the contributions by M. I. Posner, 'Cognition: Natural and Artificial', pp. 167–74 and L. E. Bourne, 'Some Forms of Cognition', pp. 313–24; and the discussions at pp. 175–87 and 325–37.

16. Quoted by A. L. Blumenthal, *The Process of Cognition* (Englewood Cliffs: Prentice-Hall, 1977) p. iv.

17. Ibid.

18. H. Tajfel and C. Fraser (eds), *Introducing Social Psychology* (Harmondsworth: Penguin, 1978) pp. 25–6.

19. Ibid, p. 25.

20. J. Moore, 'On Mentalism, Methodological Behaviourism and Radical Behaviourism', *Behaviourism*, vol. 9 (1981) p. 62.

21. E. C. Tolman, *Purposive Behaviour* (New York: Century, 1932).

22. Tolman had more fundamental differences with the behaviourists; these stemmed from his belief that learning need not be predicated upon the existence of a reinforcing state of affairs. Since learning depended upon cognition and the establishment of 'meanings', the role of reinforcers was merely to consolidate previously acquired learning.

23. C. L. Hull, *Principles of Behaviour* (New York: Century, 1943).

24. For example, K. Koffka, *Principles of Gestalt Psychology* (New York: Harcourt, Brace and World, 1935).

25. Jones and Gerard, *Foundations of Social Psychology*, p. 46.

26. T. N. Newcomb, R. H. Turner and P. E. Converse, *Social Psychology* (New York: Holt, 1965) p. 27.

27. V. Neisser, *Cognitive Psychology* (Englewood Cliffs: Prentice-Hall, 1967). The following paragraph draws upon this source. See also Koffka, *Principles of Gestalt Psychology* (London: Routledge, 1935).

28. Neisser, *Cognitive Psychology*, p. 4.

29. Ibid.

30. This account draws upon Blumenthal, *The Process of Cognition* (Englewood Cliffs: Prentice-Hall, 1977) ch. 1; and R. C. Atkinson and R. M. Shiffrin, 'The Control of Short-Term Memory', *Scientific American*, 225, no. 2 (1971) pp. 82–90.

31. Ibid.

32. A. Newell, J. C. Shaw and H. A. Simon, 'Elements of a Theory of Human Problem Solving', *Psychological Review*, vol. 65 (1958) pp. 151–66; P. H. Lindsay and P. A. Norman, *Human Information Processing* (New York: Academic Press, 1978) pp. 593–605.

33. Neisser, *Cognitive Psychology*, p.6.

34. G. R. Bower, 'A Selective Review of Organisational Factors in Memory' in E. Tulving and W. Donaldson (eds), *Organisation of Memory* (New York: Academic Press, 1972) p. 108.

35. For example, P. Kotler, *Marketing Management*, 4th edn (Englewood

Cliffs: Prentice-Hall, 1980) ch. 18; J. F. Engel, R. D. Blackwell and D. T. Kollat, *Consumer Behaviour*, 3rd edn (Hindsdale, Illinois: Dryden, 1978) ch. 16.

36.   C. I. Hovland and I. L. Janis (eds), *Personality and Persuasibility* (New Haven: Yale University Press, 1959); C. I. Hovland, I. L. Janis and H. Kelley, *Communication and Persuasion* (New Haven: Yale University Press, 1953); I. L. Janis and C. I. Hovland, 'An Overview of Persuasibility Research', in Hovland and Janis (eds), *Personality and Persuasibility* (1959) pp. 1–26.

37.   A. R. Andreasen, 'Attitudes and Customer Behaviour: A Decision Model', in L. E. Preston (ed.), *New Research in Marketing* (Berkeley: University of California, 1965) pp. 1–16.

38.   F. M. Nicosia, *Consumer Decision Processes*, (Englewood Cliffs: Prentice-Hall, 1966); 'Advertising Management, Consumer Behaviour and Simulation', *Journal of Advertising Research*, vol. 8, no. 5 (1968) pp. 233–7.

39.   J. Howard and J. N. Sheth, *The Theory of Buyer Behaviour* (New York: Wiley, 1969).

40.   Engel, Blackwell and Kollat, *Consumer Behaviour*.

41.   Engel, Blackwell and Kollat, *Consumer Behaviour*; W. J. M. McGuire, 'Some Internal Psychological Factors Influencing Consumer Choice', *Journal of Consumer Research*, vol. 2 no. 4 (1976) pp. 314–16.

42.   McGuire, 'Some Internal Psychological Factors Influencing Consumer Choice', pp. 314–16; D. A. Booth, 'Preference as a Motive', in J. H. A. Kroeze, *Preference Behaviour and Chemoreception* (Horst, The Netherlands: European Chemoreception Research Organisation, 1979) pp. 317–34.

42.   A. S. C. Ehrenberg and G. J. Goodhardt, *How Advertising Works* (New York: J. Walter Thompson/Market Research Corporation of America, 1980) p. 1.

44.   P. Zimbardo and E. B. Ebbesen, *Influencing Attitudes and Changing Behaviour* (Reading, Mass: Addison-Wesley, 1970) pp. 20–3. For a critical assessment, see M. Fishbein and I. Ajzen, *Belief, Attitude, Intention and Behaviour* (Reading, Mass: Addison-Wesley, 1975) pp. 451–7.

45.   J. N. Axelrod, 'Attitude Measures that Predict Purchase', *Journal of Advertising Research*, vol. 8, no. 1 (1968) pp. 3–17.

46.   B. Roper, 'The Importance of Attitudes, the Difficulty of Measurement', in J. S. Wright and J. Goldstrucker (eds), *New Ideas for Successful Marketing* (Chicago: American Marketing Association, 1966); T. S. Robertson, *Innovative Behaviour and Communication* (New York: Holt, 1971); C. Pinson and E. L. Roberto, 'Do Attitude Changes Precede Behaviour Change?', *Journal of Advertising Research*, vol. 13, no. 4, 1973) pp. 33–8.

47.   A. S. C. Ehrenberg and G. J. Goodhardt, *Models of Change* (New York: J. Walter Thompson/Market Research Corporation of America, 1979) pp. 12–14. See also A. S. C. Ehrenberg, 'Repetitive Advertising and the Consumer', *Journal of Advertising Research*, vol. 14, no. 2 (1974) pp. 25–34.

48.   A. S. C. Ehrenberg and G. J. Goodhardt, *Consumer Attitudes* (New York: J. Walter Thompson/Market Research Corporation of America, 1980) p. 6.

49.   W. R. Nord and J. P. Peter, 'A Behaviour Modification Perspective on Marketing', *Journal of Marketing*, vol. 44, no. 2, (1980) pp. 36–47; M. L.

Rothschild and W. C. Gaidis, 'Behavioural Learning Theory: Its Relevance to Marketing and Promotions', *Journal of Marketing*, vol. 45, no. 1 (1981) pp. 70–8.

50. Hull, *Principles of Behaviour*; L. W. Doob, 'The Behaviour of Attitudes', *Psychological Review*, vol. 54 (1947) pp. 135–56; Fishbein and Ajzen, *Belief, Attitude, Intention and Behaviour*, pp. 22–33; S. Himmelfarb and A. H. Eagly, *Readings in Attitude Change* (New York: Wiley, 1974) pp. 29–52.

51. A. W. Staats, *Social Behaviourism* (Homewood, Illinois: Dorsey, 1975); A. Bandura, 'The Self-System in Reciprocal Determinism', *American Psychologist*, vol. 33 (1978) pp. 344–58.

52. B. F. Skinner, *Science and Human Behaviour* (New York: Macmillan, 1953) pp. 73–4.

53. Skinner, *About Behaviourism*, p. 3.

54. G. A. Miller, *Psychology* (Harmondsworth: Penguin, 1962) p. 83.

55. I. P. Pavlov, *Conditioned Reflexes* (London: Oxford University Press, 1927).

56. A. W. Staats and C. K. Staats, *Complex Human Behaviour* (New York: Holt, 1963) pp. 35–41.

57. B. F. Skinner, *Beyond Freedom and Dignity* (Harmondsworth: Penguin, 1973) p. 23.

58. Skinner, *About Behaviourism*, pp. 39–40.

59. Ibid, p. 46.

60. Skinner, *Beyond Freedom and Dignity*, p. 24.

61. Ibid.

62. Skinner, *About Behaviourism*, p. 148.

63. B. F. Skinner, 'The Experimental Analysis of Operant Behaviour' in R. W. Rieber and K. Salzinger (eds), *The Roots of American Psychology* (New York: New York Academy of Sciences, 1977) p. 381. See also Staats and Staats, *Complex Human Behaviour*, pp. 77–86 and S. J. Rachman and C. Philips, *Psychology and Medicine* (Harmondsworth: Penguin, 1978) pp. 140–41, 154, 179.

64. Bandura, 'The Self–System in Reciprocal Determinism'.

65. J. Howard, *Marketing Theory* (Boston, Mass.: Allyn & Bacon, 1965).

66. For example, A. A. Kuehn, 'Consumer Brand Choice – A Learning Process?', *Journal of Advertising Research*, vol. 2, no. 6 (1962) pp. 10–17.

67. The following discussion draws upon and extends the introductions to the application of behaviourism to marketing provided by Nord and Peter, and Rothschild and Gaidis.

68. Skinner, *About Behaviourism*, p. 58; B. F. Skinner, *Reflections on Behaviourism and Society* (Englewood Cliffs: Prentice-Hall, 1978) pp. 163–70.

69. C. A. Scott, 'The Effects of Trial and Incentives on Repeat Purchase Behaviour', *Journal of Marketing Research*, vol. 13, no. 3 (1976) pp. 263–9.

70. Rothschild and Gaidis, 'Behavioural Learning Theory: Its Relevance to Marketing Promotions', p. 77.

71. A. Bandura and R. H. Walters, *Social Learning and Personality Development* (New York: Holt, 1963); A. Bandura, *Principles of Behaviour Modification* (New York: Holt, 1969).

72. Zimbardo and Ebbesen, *Influencing Attitudes and Changing Behaviour*, p. 92.

73. Blumenthal, *The Process of Cognition*, p. viii.

74. Neisser, *Cognitive Psychology*, p. 5.

75. D. P. Cushman and R. D. McPhee, *Message–Attitude–Behaviour Relationship* (New York: Academic Press, 1980) p. 7.

76. Skinner, 'The Experimental Analysis of Operant Behaviour', p. 379.

77. Jacoby, 'Consumer Research: A State of the Art Review', *Journal of Marketing*, vol. 42, no. 2 (1978) p. 337.

CHAPTER 3

1. M. Fishbein and I. Ajzen, *Belief, Attitude, Intention and Behaviour* (Reading, Mass: Addison-Wesley, 1975) p. 6.

2. L. Festinger, *A Theory of Cognitive Dissonance*, (Stanford, California: Stanford University Press, 1957); M. J. Rosenberg, 'An Analysis of Affective–Cognitive Consistency', in C. I. Hovland and M. J. Rosenberg (eds), *Attitude Organisation and Change* (New Haven: Yale University Press, 1960) pp. 15–64; M. J. Rosenberg, 'Cognitive Structure and Attitudinal Effect', *Journal of Abnormal and Social Psychology*, vol. 53, (1956) pp. 367–72; F. Heider, 'Attitudes and Cognitive Organisation', *Journal of Psychology*, vol. 21 (1946) pp. 107–12; C. E. Osgood and P. H. Tannenbaum, 'The Principle of Congruity in the Prediction of Attitude Change', *Psychological Review*, vol. 62 (1955) pp. 42–55.

3. A. W. Staats, *Social Behaviourism* (Homewood, Illinois: Dorsey, 1975); A. Bandura, 'The Self-System in Reciprocal Determinism' *American Psychologist*, vol. 33 (1978) pp. 344–58; I. Ajzen and M. Fishbein, *Understanding Attitudes and Predicting Social Behaviour* (Englewood Cliffs: Prentice-Hall, 1980); Hovland, Janis and Kelley, *Communication and Persuasion; R. F. Weiss, 'An Extension of Hullian Learning Theory to Persuasive Communication', in A. G. Greenwald (ed.), *Psychological Foundations of Attitudes* (New York: Academic Press, 1968) pp. 109–45; D. J. Bem, 'An Experimental Analysis of Self-Persuasion', *Journal of Experimental Social Psychology*, vol. 1 (1965) pp. 199–218; D. J. Bem, 'Self-Perception: An Alternative Interpretation of Cognitive Dissonance Phenomena', *Psychological Review*, vol. 74 (1967) pp. 183–200.

4. C. W. Sherif, M. Sherif and R. E. Nebergall, *Attitude and Attitude Change* (Philadelphia: Saunders, 1965); H. H. Kelley, 'Attribution Theory in Social Psychology', *Nebraska Symposium on Motivation*, vol. 15 (1967) pp. 192–238; D. Katz, 'The Functional Approach to the Study of Attitudes', *Public Opinion Quarterly*, vol. 24, (1960) pp. 163–204; H. C. Kelman, 'Compliance, Identification and Internalisation', *Journal of Conflict Resolution*, vol. 2 (1958), pp. 51–60.

5. For commentary and evaluation, see S. Himmelfarb and A. H. Eagly, *Readings in Attitude Change* (New York: Wiley, 1974) pp. 9–47; Fishbein and Ajzen, *Belief, Attitude, Intention and Behaviour*, pp. 22–50; C. A. Insko, *Theories of Attitude Change* (New York: Appleton-Century-Crofts, 1967); see also the periodic reviews in the *Annual Review of Psychology* such as: M. Fishbein and I. Ajzen, 'Attitudes and Opinion', vol. 23 (1972) pp. 487–544; C. A. Kiesler and P. A. Munson, 'Attitudes and Opinions', vol. 26 (1975), pp. 415–66; A. H.

Eagly and S. Himmelfarb, 'Attitudes and Opinions', vol. 29 (1978) pp. 517–54; R. B. Cialdini, R. E. Petty and J. T. Cacioppo, 'Attitude and Attitude Change', vol. 32 (1981) pp. 357–404.

6. D. R. Seibold, 'Attitude–Verbal Report–Behaviour Relationships as Causal Processes: Formalisation, Test, and Communication Implications' in Cushman and McPhee (eds) *Message–Attitude–Behaviour Relationship* (New York: Academic Press, 1980) pp. 195–244; R. P. Bagozzi and R. E. Burnkrant, 'Attitude Organisation and the Attitude–Behaviour Relationship', *Journal of Personality and Social Psychology*, vol. 37, no. 6 (1979) pp. 913–29; R. P. Bagozzi, A. M. Tybout, C. S. Craig and B. Sternthal, 'The Construct Validity of the Tripartite Classification of Attitudes', *Journal of Marketing Research*, vol. 16, no. 1 (1979) pp. 88–95; Ajzen and Fishbein, *Understanding Attitudes and Predicting Social Behaviour*.

7. M. L. DeFleur and F. R. Westie, 'Attitude as a Scientific Concept', *Social Forces*, vol. 42, no. 1 (1963) pp. 17–31.

8. Ibid, p.21.

9. Ibid, p.21.

10. K. Thomas (ed.), *Attitudes and Behaviour* (Harmondsworth: Penguin, 1971) p. 9.

11. B. Reich and C. Adcock, *Values, Attitudes and Behaviour Change* (London: Methuen, 1976) pp. 12–13.

12. C. Walters, *Consumer Behaviour* (Homewood, Illinois: Irwin, 1978) p. 266.

13. G. S. Day, 'Attitudes and Attitude Change' in H. H. Kassarjian and T. S. Robertson, *Perspectives in Consumer Behaviour* (London: Scott, Foresman, 1973) pp. 188–209.

14. G. W. Allport, 'Attitudes', in C. Murchison (ed.), *Handbook of Social Psychology* (Worcester, Mass: Clark University Press, 1935) pp. 798–844.

15. Kiesler, Collins and Miller state that 'the properly pedantic title for this section [of their book] should be something like "The Relationship Between Certain Kinds of Behaviour, Arbitrarily Designated by Most Social Scientists as Measures of Attitude, and Other Kinds of Behaviour, which, According to Theory, Should be Influenced by the Attitude in Question".' See C. A. Kiesler, B. E. Collins and N. Miller, *Attitude Change* (New York: Wiley, 1969) p. 23; C. A. Kiesler, *The Psychology of Commitment* (New York: Academic Press, 1971) ch. 1. The distinction between 'verbal' and 'overt' behaviours is not entirely satisfactory in this context since verbal behaviour is itself overt; the distinction has, however, been retained in this chapter simply for ease of exposition.

16. DeFleur and Westie, 'Attitude as a Scientific Concept', p. 30.

17. C. N. Alexander, 'Attitude as a Scientific Concept', *Social Forces*, vol. 45 (1966–7) pp. 278–81. The reference is to Skinner's *Science and Human Behaviour* (New York: Macmillan, 1953).

18. G. Zaltman, C. R. A. Pinson and R. Angelman, *Metatheory and Consumer Research* (New York: Holt, 1973) p. 125; G. Zaltman, 'The Structure and Purpose of Marketing Models', in F. M. Nicosia and Y. Wind (eds), *Behavioural Models for Market Analysis* (Hindsdale, Illinois: Dryden, 1977) pp. 25–40. Covariance merely represents the least evidence required if the latent pro-

cess view is to be upheld; of itself it represents the simplest notion of causality, a necessary but insufficient criterion.

19. L. R. Kahle and J. J. Berman, 'Attitudes Cause Behaviour: A Cross-Lagged Panel Analysis', *Journal of Personality and Social Psychology*, vol. 37, no. 3, (1979) pp. 315–2⅃.

20. Ibid. See also P. M. Bentler and G. Speckart, 'Attitudes "Cause" Behaviour: A Structural Equation Analysis', *Journal of Personality and Social Psychology*, vol. 40, no. 2 (1981) pp. 226–38.

21. A. Cohen, *Attitude Change and Social Influence* (New York: Basic Books, 1964) p. 138.

22. R. T. LaPiere, 'Attitudes vs. Actions', *Social Forces*, vol. 13 (1934) pp. 230–37.

23. A. W. Wicker, 'Attitudes vs. Actions: The Relationship of Verbal and Overt Responses to Attitude Objects', *Journal of Social Issues*, vol. 25 (1969) pp. 41–78.

24. L. L. Thurstone, 'The Measurement of Social Attitudes', *Journal of Abnormal and Social Psychology*, vol. 26 (1931) pp. 249–69; R. Likert, 'A Technique for the Measurement of Attitudes', *Archives of Psychology*, no. 140 (1932) (monograph); C. E. Osgood, G. J. Suci and P. H. Tannenbaum, *The Measurement of Meaning* (Urbana: University of Illinois Press, 1957).

25. A. W. Wicker, 'Attitudes vs. Actions: The Relationship of Verbal and Overt Responses to Attitude Objects', p. 53.

26. M. Fishbein, 'The Search for Attitudinal–Behavioural Consistency' in H. H. Kassarjian and T. S. Robertson (eds), *Perspectives in Consumer Behaviour* (London: Scott, Foresman, 1973, 1981); J. A. Lunn, 'A Review of Consumer Decision Process Models' (Amsterdam: ESOMAR Conference Papers, 1971); G. R. Foxall, 'Marketing Models of Buyer Behaviour', *European Research*, vol. 8, no 5 (1980) pp. 195–206; R. P. Abelson, 'Are Attitudes Necessary?', in B. T. King and E. McGinnies (eds), *Attitudes, Conflict and Social Change* (New York: Academic Press, 1972).

27. I. Ajzen and M. Fishbein, 'Attitude–Behaviour Relations: A Theoretical Analysis and Review of Empirical Research', *Psychological Bulletin*, vol. 84 (1977) pp. 888–918; Cialdini, Petty and Cacioppo, 'Attitude and Attitude Change'; Eagly, Kiesler and Munson, 'Attitudes and Opinions'; H. Schuman and M. P. Johnson, 'Attitudes and Behaviour', *Annual Review of Sociology*, vol. 2 (1976) pp. 161–207.

28. Schuman and Johnson, 'Attitudes and Behaviour', p. 199.

29. Siebold, 'Attitude–Verbal Report–Behaviour Relationships as Causal Processes: Formalisation, Test, and Communication Implications', pp. 213–14.

30. DeFleur and Westie, 'Attitude as a Scientific Concept', p. 30. Cf. N. C. Weissberg, 'Commentary on DeFleur and Westie', *Social Forces*, vol. 43 (1964-5) pp. 422–5.

31. Wicker, 'Attitudes vs. Actions: The Relationship of Verbal and Overt Responses to Attitude Objects'.

32. Kiesler, Collins and Miller, *Attitude Change;* S. J. Gross and C. M. Niman, 'Attitude–Behaviour Consistency: A Review', *Public Opinion Quarterly*, vol. 39, no. 3 (1975) pp. 358–68; C. R. Tittle and R. J. Hill, 'Attitude

Measurement and Prediction of Behaviour', *Sociometry*, vol. 30 (1967) pp. 199–213; C. R. Tittle and R. J. Hill, 'The Accuracy of Self-Reported Data and Prediction of Political Activity', *Public Opinion Quarterly*, vol. 31 (1967) pp. 103–6.

33. Seibold, 'Attitude–Verbal Report–Behaviour Relationships as Causal Processes', p. 221.

34. Schuman and Johnson, 'Attitudes and Behaviour', p. 164, p. 200.

35. Ajzen and Fishbein, 'Attitude–Behaviour Relations: A Theoretical Analysis and Review of Empirical Research', pp. 889–92.

36. Seibold, 'Attitude–Verbal Report–Behaviour Relationships: Formalisation, Test, and Communication Implications', p. 221.

37. Ibid.

38. Wicker, 'Attitudes vs. Actions: 'The Relationship of Verbal and Overt Responses to Attitude Objects', p. 76.

39. Ibid, p. 75.

40. Fishbein and Ajzen, *Belief, Attitude, Intention and Behaviour;* Ajzen and Fishbein, *Understanding Attitudes and Predicting Social Behaviour*; see also P. Sampson and P. Harris, 'A User's Guide to Fishbein', *Journal of the Market Research Society*, vol. 12, no. 3 (1970) pp. 145–62.

41. D. E. Dulany, 'Awareness, Rules and Propositional Control', in D. Horton and T. Dixon (eds) *Verbal Behaviour and S–R Behaviour Theory* (Englewood Cliffs: Prentice-Hall, 1968) pp. 340–87; Rosenberg, 'Cognitive Structure and Attitudinal Effect'.

42. M. Fishbein, 'Attitude and the Prediction of Behaviour', in M. Fishbein (ed.), *Readings in Attitude Theory and Measurement* (New York: Wiley, 1967) pp. 377–92; M. Tuck, *How Do We Choose?* (London: Methuen, 1976); W. L. Wilkie and E. A. Pessemier, 'Issues in Marketing's Use of Multi-Attribute Attitude Models', *Journal of Marketing*, vol. 10, no. 4 (1973) pp. 428–41.

43. I. Ajzen and M. Fishbein, 'Attitudinal and Normative Variables as Predictors of Specific Behaviours', *Journal of Personality and Social Psychology*, vol. 27 (1973) pp. 41–57; Fishbein and Ajzen, 'Attitudes and Opinions'.

44. I. Ajzen and M. Fishbein, 'Attitudinal and Normative Variables as Predictors of Specific Behaviours', *Journal of Personality and Social Psychology*, vol. 27 (1973) pp. 41–57.

45. R. P. Schlegel, C. A. Crawford and M. D. Sandburn, 'Correspondence and Mediational Properties of the Fishbein Model', *Journal of Experimental Social Psychology*, vol. 13 (1977) pp. 421–30; K. M. Kitty, 'Attitudinal and Normative Variables as Predictors of Drinking Behaviour', *Journal of Studies in Alcoholism*, vol. 39 (1978) pp. 1178–94.

46. C. H. Bowman and M. Fishbein, 'Understanding Public Reaction to Energy Proposals', *Journal of Applied Social Psychology*, vol. 8 (1978) pp. 319–40.

47. D. Vinokur-Kaplan, 'To Have or Not-to-Have Another Child', *Journal of Applied Social Psychology*, vol. 8 (1978) pp. 29–46.

48. P. Hom, R. Katerberg and C. L. Hullin, 'Comparative Examination of Three Approaches to the Prediction of Turnover', *Journal of Applied Psychology*, vol. 64 (1979) pp. 280–90.

49. I. Ajzen and M. Fishbein, 'Attitudes and Normative Beliefs as Factors Influencing Behavioural Intentions', *Journal of Personality and Social Psychology*, vol. 21 (1972) pp. 1–9. See also M. Fishbein, 'The Prediction of Behaviour

from Attitudinal Variables', in C. D. Mortensen and K. K. Sereno (eds), *Advances in Communications Research* (New York: Harper & Row, 1973) pp. 3–31.

50. D. T. Wilson, H. L. Matthews and J. W. Harvey, 'An Empirical Test of the Fishbein Behavioural Intention Model', *Journal of Consumer Research*, vol. 1, no. 4 (1975) p. 40.

51. Ibid.

52. Schuman and Johnson, 'Attitudes and Behaviour', pp. 172–3.

53. M. J. Ryan and E. H. Bonfield, 'Fishbein's Intentions Model: A Test of External and Pragmatic Validity', *Journal of Marketing*, vol. 44, no. 2 (1980) pp. 82–95.

54. Ibid.

55. M. A. Ryan and E. H. Bonfield, 'The Fishbein Extended Model and Consumer Behaviour', *Journal of Consumer Research*, vol. 2, no. 2 (1975) pp. 118–36.

56. G. D. Harrell and P. D. Bennett, 'An Evaluation of the Expectancy Value Model of Attitude Measurement for Physician Prescribing Behaviour', *Journal of Marketing Research*, vol. 11, no. 4 (1974) pp. 269–78.

57. E. H. Bonfield, 'Attitudes, Social Influence, Personal Norm and Intention Interactions as Related to Brand Purchase Behaviour', *Journal of Marketing Research*, vol. 11, no. 4 (1974) pp. 379–89. Ryan and Bonfield, 'Fishbein's Intentions Model: A Test of External and Pragmatic Validity'.

58. A. W. Wicker, 'An Examination of the "Other Variables" Explanation of Attitude-Behaviour Inconsistency', *Journal of Personality and Social Psychology*, vol. 19 (1971) pp. 18–30.

59. W. F. van Raaij, 'Economic Psychology', *Journal of Economic Psychology*, vol. 1, no. 1 (1981), pp. 1–24.

60. Ibid, p.11.

61. M. Rokeach, *Beliefs, Attitudes and Values* (San Francisco: Jossey-Bass, 1969); see also 'Attitude Change and Behaviour Change', *Public Opinion Quarterly*, vol. 30 (1967) pp. 529–50.

62. Fishbein, 'The Search for Attitudinal–Behavioural Consistency'.

63. Ibid, p.256.

64. P. W. Miniard and J. B. Cohen, 'Isolating Attitudinal and Normative Influences in Behavioural Intentions Models', *Journal of Marketing Research*, vol. 16, no. 1 (1979) pp. 102–10.

65. J. N. Sheth, 'A Field Study of Attitude Structure and the Attitude–Behaviour Relationship', in J. N. Sheth (ed.), *Models of Buyer Behaviour* (New York: Harper & Row, 1974) pp. 242–68.

66. Ibid, p.250.

67. Ibid, pp. 250–1.

68. J. F. Engel, R. D. Blackwell and D. T. Kollat, *Consumer Behaviour*, 3rd edn (Hindsdale, Illinois: Dryden, 1978) pp. 403–4.

69. Sheth, 'A Field Study of Attitude Structure and the Attitude-Behaviour Relationship'.

70. Ibid.

71. Schuman and Johnson, 'Attitudes and Behaviour'.

72. W. O. Bearden and A. G. Woodside, 'Interactions of Consumption Situations and Brand Attitudes', *Journal of Applied Psychology*, vol. 61, no. 6 (1976), pp. 764–9.

73. A. S. C. Ehrenberg and G. J. Goodhardt, *Consumer Attitudes* (New

York: J. Walter Thompson/Market Research Corporation of America, 1980) p. 20.

74. Ibid. See also B. F. Skinner, *Verbal Behaviour* (New York: Appleton-Century-Crofts, 1957).

75. DeFleur and Westie, 'Attitude as a Scientific Concept', p. 27.

76. Ehrenberg and Goodhardt, *Consumer Attitudes*, pp. 21–2.

77. Fishbein, 'Attitude and the Prediction of Behaviour'.

78. Festinger, *A Theory of Cognitive Dissonance.*

79. Bem, 'An Experimental Analysis of Self-Persuasion'.

80. D. J. Bem and A. Allen, 'On Predicting Some of the People Some of the Time: The Search for Cross-Situational Consistencies in Behaviour', *Psychological Review,* vol. 81 (1974) pp. 506–20.

81. H. C. Triandis, *Interpersonal Behaviour* (Monterey: Brooks-Cole, 1977). See also H. C. Triandis, 'Exploratory Factor Analyses of the Behavioural Component of Social Attitudes', *Journal of Abnormal and Social Psychology,* vol. 68 (1964) pp. 420–30.

82. R. P. Bagozzi, 'Attitudes, Intentions and Behaviour: A Test of Some Key Hypotheses', *Journal of Personality and Social* Psychology, vol. 41, no. 4 (1981) pp. 607–27. See also R. P. Bagozzi, 'A Field Investigation of Causal Relations Among Cognitions, Affect, Intentions and Behaviour', *Journal of Marketing Research,* vol. 19, no. 4 (1982); and R. P. Bagozzi, 'An Examination of the Validity of Two Models of Attitude', *Multivariate Behavioural Research,* vol. 16 (1981) pp. 323–59.

83. Fishbein and Ajzen, *Belief, Attitude, Intention and Behaviour.*

84. Dulany, 'Awareness, Rules and Propositional Control'.

85. Wicker, 'Attitudes vs. Actions: The Relationship of Verbal and Overt Responses to Attitude Objects'.

CHAPTER 4

1. P. M. Bentler, 'Multivariate Analysis with Latent Variables: Causal Modeling', *Annual Review of Psychology,* vol. 31, (1980) pp. 419–56.

2. H. H. Kassarjian, 'Presidential Address, 1977: Anthropomorphism and Parsimony', in *Advances in Consumer Research,* vol. 5 (Chicago: Association for Consumer Research, 1978) pp. xiii–xiv.

3. For example, M. B. Holbrook, 'Comparing Multi-Attribute Attitude Models by Optimal Scaling', *Journal of Consumer Research,* vol. 4, no. 3 (1977) pp. 165–71; A. V. Bruno and A. R. Wildt, 'Toward Understanding Attitude Structure: A Study of the Complementarity of Multi-Attribute Attitude Models', *Journal of Consumer Research,* vol. 2, no. 2 (1975) pp. 137–45; M. B. Mazis, O. T. Ahtola and R. E. Klippel, 'A Comparison of Four Multi-Attribute Models in the Prediction of Consumer Attitudes', *Journal of Consumer Research,* vol. 2, no. 1 (1975) pp. 38–52; J. J. Bernado and J. M. Blin, 'A Programming Model of Consumer Choice Among Multi-Attributed Brands', *Journal of Consumer Research,* vol. 4, no. 2 (1977) pp. 111–118; J. R. Bettman, N. Capon and R. J. Lutz, 'Multi-Attribute Measurement Models and Multi-Attribute Attitude Theory: A Test of Construct Validity', *Journal of Consumer Research,* vol. 1, no. 4

(1975) pp. 1–15; cf. J. Shanteau and C. M. Troutman, 'Commentary', *Journal of Consumer Research*, vol. 1, no. 4 (1975) pp. 16–18; and G. Wolf, 'Commentary', *Journal of Consumer Research*, vol. 1, no. 4 (1975) pp. 18–19.

4. For example, D. J. Reibstein, 'The Prediction of Individual Probabilities of Brand Choice', *Journal of Consumer Research*, vol. 5, no. 3 (1978) pp. 163–8; A. R. Wildt and A. V. Bruno, 'The Prediction of Preference for Capital Equipment Using Linear Attitude Models', *Journal of Marketing Research*, vol. 11, no. 2 (1974) pp. 203–5.

5. R. J. Lutz, 'Changing Brand Attitudes Through Modification of Cognitive Structure', *Journal of Consumer Research*, vol. 1, no. 4 (1975) pp. 49–59.

6. For example, J. Jaccard, 'Toward Theories of Persuasion and Belief Change', *Journal of Personality and Social Psychology*, vol. 40, no. 2 (1981) pp. 260–9; R. R. Dholakia, 'Influencing Buyer Behaviour', *European Journal of Marketing*, vol. 13 (1979) pp. 282–93.

7. T. V. Bonoma and W. J. Johnston, 'Decision Making Under Uncertainty: A Direct Measurement Approach', *Journal of Consumer Research*, vol. 6, no. 2 (1979) pp. 177–91.

8. For example, R. J. Lutz, 'An Experimental Investigation of Causal Relations Among Cognitions, Affect and Behavioural Intention', *Journal of Consumer Research*, vol. 3, no. 4 (1977) pp. 197–208; P. R. Dickson and P. W. Miniard, 'A Further Examination of Two Laboratory Tests of the Extended Fishbein Attitude Model', *Journal of Consumer Research*, vol. 4, no. 4 (1978) pp. 261–6; Carnegie-Mellon University Marketing Seminar, 'Attitude Change or Attitude Formation? An Unanswered Question', *Journal of Consumer Research*, vol. 4, no. 4 (1978) pp. 271–6; see also Lutz's rejoinders in the same issue, pp. 266–71 and 276–8. D. J. Reibstein, C. H. Lovelock and R. de P. Dobson, 'The Direction of Causality Between Perceptions, Affect, and Behaviour: An Application to Travel Behaviour', *Journal of Consumer Research*, vol. 6, no. 4 (1980) pp. 370–76; J. L. Ginter, 'An Experimental Investigation of Attitude Change and Choice of a New Brand', *Journal of Marketing Research*, vol. 11, no. 1 (1974) pp. 30–40.

9. For example, J. Jacoby, D. E. Speller and C. A. Kohn, 'Brand Choice as a Function of Information Load', *Journal of Marketing Research*, vol. 11, no. 1 (1974) pp. 63–9.

10. M. Tuck, 'Fishbein Theory and the Bass-Talarzk Problem', *Journal of Marketing Research*, vol. 10, no. 3 (1973) pp. 345–8.

11. P. Sampson and P. Harris, 'A User's Guide to Fishbein', *Journal of the Market Research Society*, vol. 12, no. 3 (1970) pp. 145–62.

12. Tuck, 'Fishbein Theory', p. 347.

13. Lutz, 'Changing Brand Attitudes Through Modification of Cognitive Structure'; 'An Experimental Investigation of Causal Relations Among Cognitions, Affect and Behavioural Intention'.

14. R. J. Lutz, 'An Experimental Investigation of Causal Relations Among Cognitions, Affect, and Behavioural Intention', *Journal of Consumer Research*, vol. 3, no. 4 (1977) p. 206.

15. Dickson and Miniard, 'A Further Examination of Two Laboratory Tests of the Extended Fishbein Attitude Model'.

16. L. Festinger, *A Theory of Cognitive Dissonance* (Stanford, California: Stanford University Press, 1957).

17. H. E. Krugman, 'The Impact of Television Advertising: Learning without Involvement', *Public Opinion Quarterly*, vol. 29 (1965) pp. 349–55; 'Brain Wave Measurements of Media Involvement', *Journal of Advertising Research*, vol. 11, no. 1 (1971) pp. 3–9; 'Why Three Exposures may be Enough', *Journal of Advertising Research*, vol. 12, no. 6 (1972) pp. 11–14; 'Memory Without Recall, Exposure Without Perception', *Journal of Advertising Research*, vol. 17, no. 4 (1977) pp. 7–12.

18. D. J. Bem, 'Self-perception: An Alternative Interpretation of Cognitive Dissonance Phenomena', *Psychological Review*, vol. 74 (1967) pp. 188–200.

19. Dickson and Miniard, 'A Further Examination of Two Laboratory Tests of the Extended Fishbein Attitude Model.

20. R. J. Lutz, 'Rejoinder', *Journal of Consumer Research*, vol. 4, no. 4 (1978) pp. 266–71, 276–8.

21. Ginter, 'An Experimental Investigation of Attitude Change and Choice of New Brand'.

22. Reibstein, Lovelock and Dobson, 'The Direction of Causality Between Perceptions, Affect, and Behaviour: An Application to Travel Behaviour', p. 374.

23. R. P. Bagozzi, 'An Examination of the Validity of Two Models of Attitude', *Multivariate Behavioural Research*, vol. 16 (1981) p. 357.

24. Ibid, p. 356.

25. Jacoby, Speller and Kohn, 'Brand Choice as a Function of Information Load'; J. Jacoby, R. W. Chestnut and W. Silberman, 'Consumer Use and Comprehension of Nutrition Information', *Journal of Consumer Research*, vol. 4, no. 2 (1977) pp. 119–28; J. Jacoby, R. W. Chestnut and W. A. Fisher, 'A Behavioural Process Approach to Information Acquisition in Nondurable Purchasing', *Journal of Marketing Research*, vol. 15, no. 4 (1978) pp. 532–44.

26. J. R. Bettman and P. Kakkar, 'Effects of Information Presentation Format on Consumer Information Acquisition Strategies', *Journal of Consumer Research*, vol. 3, no. 4 (1977) pp. 233–40.

27. Jacoby, Chestnut and Silberman, 'Consumer Use and Comprehension of Nutrition Information', p. 126, emphasis original.

28. Jacoby, Speller and Kohn, 'Brand Choice as a Function of Information Load'.

29. See also Jacoby, Chestnut and Fisher, 'A Behavioural Process Approach to Information Acquisition in Nondurable Purchasing'.

30. D. L. Scammon, '"Information Load" and Consumers', *Journal of Consumer Research*, vol. 2, no. 3 (1975) pp. 148–55.

31. J. R. Bettman, 'Issues in Designing Consumer Information Environments', *Journal of Consumer Research*, vol. 2, no. 3 (1975) pp. 169–77.

32. For example, Bettman and Kakkar, 'Effects of Information Presentation Format on Consumer Information Acquisition Strategies'.

33. D. A. Lussier and R. W. Olshavsky, 'Task Complexity and Contingent Processing in Brand Choice', *Journal of Consumer Research*, vol. 6, no. 2 (1979) pp. 154–65.

34. R. E. Burnkrant, 'A Motivational Model of Information Processing Intentisy', *Journal of Consumer Research*, vol. 3, no. 1 (1976) pp. 21–30.

35. J. Jacoby, G. J. Szybillo and J. Busato-Schach, 'Information Acquisition Behaviour in Brand Choice Situations', *Journal of Consumer Research*, vol. 3, no. 4 (1977) pp. 209–16.

36. R. W. Olshavsky and D. H. Granbois, 'Consumer Decision Making – Fact or Fiction?', *Journal of Consumer Research*, vol. 6, no. 2 (1979) p. 98. See also F. Boggis and S. Broomfield, 'Problem Solving: A Dilemma in Consumer Education', *The Home Economist*, vol. 1 (1982) pp. 79–81.

37. H. A. Simon, *Administrative Behaviour* (New York: Free Press, 1957); A. Newell and H. A. Simon, *Human Problem Solving* (Englewood Cliffs: Prentice-Hall, 1972).

38. Engel, Blackwell and Kollat, *Consumer Behaviour*, 3rd edn (Hindsdale, Illinois: Dryden, 1978) pp. 242–3.

39. R. W. Hill and R. T. Hillier, *Organisational Buying Behaviour* (London: Macmillan, 1977).

40. D. H. Granbois, 'Shopping Behaviour and Preferences', in *Selected Aspects of Consumer Behaviour: A Summary from the Perspective of Different Disciplines* (Washington, D.C.: U.S. Government Printing Service, 1977) pp. 259–98.

41. J. W. Newman, 'Consumer External Search: Amount and Determinants', in A. G. Woodside, J. N. Sheth and P. D. Bennett (eds), *Consumer and Industrial Buying Behaviour* (New York: North-Holland, 1977).

42. W. Wells and L. A. LoSciuto, 'Direct Observation of Purchasing Behaviour', *Journal of Marketing Research*, vol. 3, no. 4 (1966) pp. 227–33.

43. R. E. Frank and W. F. Massy, 'Shelf Position and Space Effects', *Journal of Marketing Research*, vol. 7, no. 1 (1970) pp. 59–66; A. Gabor and C. W. J. Granger, 'On the Price Consciousness of Consumers', *Applied Statistics*, vol. 10, no. 2 (1961) pp. 170–88; J. D. McConnell, 'The Development of Brand Loyalty', *Journal of Marketing Research*, vol. 5, no. 1 (1968) pp. 13–19; R. L. Brown, 'Wrapper Influence on the Perception of Freshness in Bread', *Journal of Applied Psychology*, vol. 42, no. 4 (1958) pp. 257–60; G. R. Foxall, *Consumer Behaviour* (London: Croom Helm, and New York: Wiley, 1980) chapter 2.

44. S. Ward, 'Consumer Socialisation', *Journal of Consumer Research*, vol. 1, no. 2 (1974) pp. 1–14.

44. J. D. Thompson, *Organisations in Action* (New York: McGraw-Hill, 1967) p. 134.

45. P. H. Lindsay and P. A. Norman, *Human Information Processing*, New York: Academic Press, 1978) p. 544.

46. N. Brunsson, 'The Irrationality of Action and Action Irrationality: Decisions, Ideologies and Organisation Actions', *Journal of Management Studies*, vol. 19, no. 1 (1982) p. 35.

47. Engel, Blackwell and Kollat, *Consumer Behaviour*, p. 392.

48. Bettman, Capon and Lutz, 'Multi-Attribute Measurement Models'.

49. R. Ferber, 'Family Decision Making and Economic Behaviour', in E. B. Sheldon (ed.), *Family Economic Behaviour* (Philadelphia: Lippincott, 1973) pp. 29–61.

50. Olshavsky and Granbois, 'Consumer Decision Making – Fact or Fiction?'.

51. G. R. Foxall, 'Social Factors in Consumer Choice: Replication and Extension', *Journal of Consumer Research*, vol. 2, no. 1 (1975) pp. 60–64; reprinted in G. R. Foxall, *Marketing Behaviour* (Aldershot: Gower, 1981).

52. C. Pinson and E. L. Roberto, 'Do Attitude Changes Precede Behaviour Change?', *Journal of Advertising Research*, vol. 13, no. 4 (1973) pp. 35–8.

53. Pinson and Roberto provide these quotations which are from: T. S. Robertson, *Innovative Behaviour and Communications* (New York: Holt, 1971) pp. 66–7; Roper, 'The Importance of Attitudes, The Difficulty of Measurement', in J. S. Wright and J. Goldstrucker (eds), *New Ideas for Successful Marketing* (Chicago: American Marketing Association, 1966); J. Fothergill, 'Do Attitudes Change before Behaviour?' (ESOMAR, 1968).

54. L. Festinger, *A Theory of Cognitive Dissonance*.

55. See W. H. Cummings and M. Venkatesan, 'Cognitive Dissonance and Consumer Behaviour: A Review of the Evidence', *Journal of Marketing Research*, vol. 13, no. 3 (1976) pp. 307–8.

56. For a concise review of some studies see ibid. Most consumer behaviour texts appraise the literature on cognitive dissonance; see, for instance, G. R. Foxall, *Consumer Behaviour*, ch. 3.

57. R. B. Zajonc, 'Attitudinal Effects of Mere Exposure', *Journal of Personality and Social Psychology*, vol. 9, no. 2, part 2 (1968) pp. 92–8.

58. Ibid, p. 97.

59. G. R. Miller, 'Afterword' in Cushman and McPhee (eds), *Message–Attitude–Behaviour Relationship* (New York: Academic Press, 1980) pp. 319–27.

60. See R. P. Dholakia and B. Sternthal, 'Highly Credible Sources: Persuasive Facilitators or Persuasive Liabilities?', *Journal of Consumer Research*, vol. 3, no. 4 (1977) pp. 223–32; B. Sternthal, R. Dholakia and C. Leavitt, 'The Persuasive Effect of Source Credibility: Tests of Cognitive Response', *Journal of Consumer Research*, vol. 4, no. 4 (1978) pp. 252–60; R. P. Dhokalia, 'Influencing Buyer Behaviour', pp. 282–93.

61. W. D. Bearden and A. G. Woodside, 'Interactions of Consumption Situations and Brand Attitudes', *Journal of Applied Psychology*, vol. 61, no. 6 (1976) pp. 764–9.

62. Ibid, p. 768.

63. R. W. Belk, 'An Exploratory Assessment of Situational Effects in Buyer Behaviour', *Journal of Marketing Research*, vol. 11, no. 2 (1974) pp. 156–63; 'Situational Variables and Consumer Behaviour', *Journal of Consumer Research*, vol. 2, no. 3 (1975) pp. 157–64.

64. Belk, 'An Exploratory Assessment of Situational Effects in Buyer Behaviour', pp. 156–7.

66. R. J. Lutz and P. Kakkar, 'The Psychological Situation as a Determinant of Consumer Behaviour', in *Advances in Consumer Research*, vol. 2 (Chicago: Association for Consumer Research, 1975) p. 439; see also P. Kakkar and R. J. Lutz, 'Toward a Taxonomy of Consumption Situations', *Proceedings of the American Marketing Association* (Chicago: AMA, 1975) pp. 206–10.

67. R. W. Belk, 'Situational Mediation and Consumer Behaviour', *Journal of Consumer Research*, vol. 3, no. 3 (1976), pp. 175–7.

68. R. J. Lutz and P. Kakkar, 'Situational Influences in Interpersonal Persuasion', in *Advances in Consumer Research*, vol. 3 (Ann Arbor: Association for Consumer Research, 1976) pp. 370–8.

69. F. Hansen, *Consumer Choice Behaviour: A Cognitive Theory* (New York: Free Press, 1972); 'Psychological Theories of Consumer Choice', *Journal of Consumer Research*, vol. 3, no. 3 (1976).

70. P. Kakkar and R. J. Lutz, 'Situational Influence on Consumer Behaviour: A Review', in Kassarjian and Robertson (eds), *Perspectives in Consumer Behaviour* (Glenview: Scott, Foresman, 1981) pp. 204–15. See also Lutz and Kakkar, 'Situational Influences in Interpersonal Persuasion'.

71. Belk, 'Situational Variables and Consumer Behaviour', p. 157. See also the source of the concept of behavioural setting: R. G. Barker, *Ecological Psychology* (Stanford, California: Stanford University Press, 1968).

72. Belk, 'Situational Variables and Consumer Behaviour', p. 158.

73. Kakkar and Lutz, 'Situational Influence on Consumer Behaviour'.

74. Belk, 'An Exploratory Assessment of Situational Effects'.

75. Ibid, p. 162.

76. Lutz and Kakkar, 'Situational Influence in Interpersonal Persuasion', p. 444.

67. Belk, 'Situational Variables and Consumer Behaviour', p. 160. Cf. Lutz and Kakkar, 'Situational Influence on Consumer Behaviour', p. 207.

78. For example, J. A. Russell and A. Mehrabian, 'Environmental Variables in Consumer Research', *Journal of Consumer Research*, vol. 3, no. 1 (1976) pp. 62–3.

79. D. J. Bem, 'An Experimental Analysis of Self-Persuasion', *Journal of Experimental Social Psychology*, vol. 1 (1965) p. 199; R. A. Detweiler and M. P. Zanner, 'Psychological Mediation of Attitudinal Responses', *Journal of Personality and Social Psychology*, vol. 33, no. 1 (1976) p. 107–13; C. Hendrick and M. Giesen, 'Self Attribution of Attitude as a Function of Belief Feedback', *Memory and Cognition*, vol. 4, no. 2 (1976) pp. 150–160.

80. M. J. Baker, *Marketing New Industrial Products* (London: Macmillan, 1975) pp. 34–40.

81. J. N. Sheth, 'A Model of Industrial Buyer Behaviour', *Journal of Marketing*, vol. 37, no. 4 (1973) p. 54.

82. Kakkar and Lutz, 'Situational Influence on Consumer Behaviour', pp. 210–11.

83. D. T. Campbell, 'Social Attitudes and other Acquired Behavioural Dispositions', in S. Koch (ed.), *Psychology*, vol. 6 (New York: McGraw-Hill, 1963).

84. Bem, 'An Experimental Analysis of Self-Persuasion'; 'Self-Perception: An Alternative Interpretation of Cognitive Dissonance Phenomena' *Psychological Review*, vol. 74 (1967) pp. 183–200; 'Self-Perception Theory' in L. Berkowitz (ed.), *Advances in Experimental Social Psychology* (New York: Academic Press, 1972) pp. 1–62.

85. C. A. Scott, 'Effects of Trial and Incentives on Repeat Purchase Behaviour', *Journal of Marketing Research*, vol. 13, no. 3 (1976) p. 264.

86. C. A. Scott, 'Forming Beliefs from Experience: Evidence from Self-Perception Theory', in Kassarjian and Robertson (eds), *Perspectives in Consumer Behaviour*, pp. 296–306.

87. Scott, 'Effects of Trial and Incentive on Repeat Purchase Behaviour', p. 266.

88. Rothschild and Gaidis, 'Behavioural Learning Theory: Its Relevance to Marketing and Promotions', *Journal of Marketing*, vol. 45, No. 1 (1981) pp. 73–4.

90. J. A. Dodson, A. M. Tybout and B. Sternthal, 'Impact of Deal and

Deal Retraction on Brand Switching', *Journal of Marketing Research*, vol. 15, no. 1 (1978) p. 79.

91. Ibid, p. 80.

92. Rothschild and Gaidis, 'Behavioural Learning Theory: Its Relevance to Marketing and Promotions', p. 74.

93. A. M. Tybout, 'The Relative Effectiveness of Three Behavioural Influence Strategies as Supplements to Persuasion in a Marketing Context', *Journal of Marketing Research*, vol. 15, no. 3 (1978) pp. 229–42.

94. Dholakia, 'Influencing Buyer Behaviour'; see also: R. R. Dholakia and B. Sternthal, 'Highly Credible Sources: Persuasive Facilitators or Persuasive Liabilities?', *Journal of Consumer Research*, vol. 3, no. 4 (1977) pp. 223–32; B. Sternthal, R. Dholakia and C. Leavitt, 'The Persuasive Effect of Source Credibility: Tests of Cognitive Response', *Journal of Consumer Research*, vol. 4, no. 4 (1978) pp. 252–60.

95. Scott, 'Effects of Trial and Incentives on Repeat Purchase Behaviour', p. 263.

96. Ibid, p. 263.

97. Ibid, p. 268.

98. Bem, 'Self-Perception: An Alternative Explanation of Cognitive Dissonance Phenomena', pp. 188–9, 200.

99. Ibid, p. 194.

100. Bem, 'An Experimental Analysis of Self Persuasion', p. 216.

101. D. J. Bem, 'Attitudes as Self-Descriptors: Another Look at the Attitude Behaviour Link', in A. G. Greenwald, T. C. Brock and T. M. Ostrom (eds), *Psychological Foundations of Attitudes* (New York: Academic Press, 1968) p. 215.

102. T. S. Kuhn, 'The Function of Dogma in Scientific Research', in B. Barnes (ed.) *Sociology of Science* (Harmondsworth: Penguin, 1972) pp. 100–1.

103. J. N. Sheth, 'A Field Study of Attitude Structure and the Attitude–Behaviour Relationship', in J. N. Sheth (ed.), *Models of Buyer Behaviour* (New York: Harper & Row, 1974) p. 268.

CHAPTER 5

1. M. L. DeFleur and F. R. Westie, 'Attitude as a Scientific Concept', *Social Forces*, vol. 42, no. 1 (1963) pp. 29–30.

2. Ibid, p. 30.

3. Ibid.

4. H. E. Krugman, 'The Impact of Television Advertising: Learning without Involvement', *Public Opinion Quarterly*, vol. 29 (1965) pp. 349–55.

5. Ibid, p. 351.

6. Ibid, p. 354.

7. Cialdini, Petty and Cacioppo, 'Attitude and Attitude Change', *Annual Review of Psychology*, vol. 32 (1981) pp. 392–3.

8. Ibid, p. 365.

9. T. S. Robertson, 'Low Commitment Consumer Behaviour', *Journal of Advertising Research*, vol. 16, no. 2 (1976) pp. 19–24.

10. Ibid, p. 23.

11. Cialdini, Petty and Cacioppo, 'Attitudes and Attitude Change', pp. 365–6.

12. J. F. Engel and R. D. Blackwell, *Consumer Behaviour*, 4th edn (Hindsdale, Illinois: Dryden, 1982).

13. A. S. C. Ehrenberg, *Repeat Buying* (Amsterdam: North-Holland, 1972); 'Towards an Integrated Theory of Consumer Behaviour', *Journal of the Market Research Society*, vol. 11, no. 4 (1969) pp. 305–37.

14. Detailed consideration of the nature and relevance of the probabilistic models of consumer choice is beyond the scope of this book which is concerned with general psychological orientations to the study of consumer behaviour. See, however, A. S. C. Ehrenberg and G. J. Goodhardt, *The Dirichet Model* (J. Walter Thompson/Market Research Corporation of America, 1979); *Models of Change* (J. Walter Thompson/Market Research Corporation of America, 1979); C. Chatfield and G. J. Goodhardt, 'Results Concerning Brand Choice', *Journal of Marketing Research*, vol. 12, no. 1 (1975) pp. 110–13. For an interesting comment on behavioural science and behaviourism in marketing see F. M. Nicosia, 'Brand Choice – Toward Behavioural-Behaviourist Models', in H. L. Davies and A. J. Silk (eds), *Behavioural and Management Science in Marketing* (New York: Wiley, 1978) pp. 12–55.

15. B. F. Skinner, *About Behaviourism* (London: Cape, 1974) p. 10.

16. Ibid, p. 211.

17. B. I. Silverman and R. Cochrane, 'Effect of the Social Context on the Principle of Belief Congruence', *Journal of Personality and Social Psychology*, vol. 22, no. 2 (1972) pp. 259–65.

18. R. Norman, 'Affective Cognitive Consistency and the Attitude Behaviour Relationship', *Proceedings of the 81st Annual Convention* (Montreal: American Psychological Association, 1973) pp. 257–69.

19. I. Ajzen and M. Fishbein, 'Attitude–Behaviour Relations: A Theoretical Analysis and a Review of Empirical Research', *Psychological Bulletin*, vol. 84 (1977) p. 889.

20. B. Mostyn, *The Attitude–Behaviour Relationship* (Bradford: MCB Publications, 1978) p. 71.

21. I. Ajzen and M. Fishbein, *Understanding Attitudes and Predicting Social Behaviour* (Englewood Cliffs: Prentice-Hall, 1980) pp. 171–2.

22. Ibid.

23. M. Tuck, *How Do We Choose?* (London: Methuen, 1976).

24. H. Schuman and M. P. Johnson, 'Attitudes and Behaviour', *Annual Review of Sociology*, vol. 2 (1976) p. 172.

25. M. Fishbein and I. Ajzen, *Belief, Attitude, Intention and Behaviour* (Reading, Mass: Addison-Wesley, 1975) pp. 374–5.

26. Schuman and Johnson, 'Attitudes and Behaviour', p. 171.

27. A. S. C. Ehrenberg and G. J. Goodhardt, *Consumer Attitudes* (New York: J. Walter Thompson/Market Research Corporation of America, 1980) p. 24.

28. D. Canter and C. Kerry, 'Approaches to Environmental Evaluation', *International Review of Applied Psychology*, vol. 31, no. 2 (1982) p. 147.

29. For example, G. J. Gorn, 'The Effects of Muni in Advertising on Choice Behaviour: A Classical Conditioning Approach', *Journal of Marketing*, vol. 46, no. 1 (1982) pp. 94–101.

30. M. J. Baker, *Marketing New Industrial Products* (London: Macmillan, 1975) pp. 73–9.

31. A. Bandura, *Principles of Behaviour Modification* (New York: Holt, 1969); W. R. Nord and J. P. Peter, 'A Behaviour Modification Perspective on Marketing', *Journal of Marketing*, vol. 44, no. 2 (1980) pp. 36–47; M. J. Baker and G. A. Churchill, 'The Impact of Physically Attractive Models on Advertising Evaluations', *Journal of Marketing Research*, vol. 14, no. 4 (1977) pp. 538–55.

32. For example, P. E. Green and Y. Wind, 'A New Way to Measure Consumers' Judgments', *Harvard Business Review*, vol. 53, no. 4 (1975) pp. 107–17.

33. J. A. Dodson, A. M. Tybout and B. Sternthal, 'Impact of Deal and Deal Retraction on Brand Switching', *Journal of Marketing Research*, vol. 15, no. 1 (1978) pp. 72–81.

Index